MUSIC FACE TO FACE

MUSIC FACE TO FACE

BY

ANDRE PREVIN

AND

ANTONY HOPKINS

CHARLES SCRIBNER'S SONS
NEW YORK

A–2.72 [V]

Printed in the United States of America
Library of Congress Catalog Card Number 74-38530
SBN 684–12846–2 (trade cloth)
SBN 684–12873–X (trade cloth, SL)

PRELUDE

Antony Hopkins

THIS is a book about two careers, careers that have never
converged professionally until this point in time, but which
have certain similarities—enuogh at any rate to give it a
logical pattern. We have both preferred variety to specializa-
tion; we have both worked in films and the theatre; we have
both found versatility a blessing which can also have draw-
backs. When, therefore, I was asked by my friend Hamish
Hamilton if I would be prepared to become involved in a
book of conversations with André Previn, I agreed to do so
because I knew we would have much in common, while the
enormous differences of background, status and achieve-
ment would make for a stimulating contrast. Our discus-
sions took place during a tour in Romania; André was
conducting the London Symphony Orchestra in concerts
in Bucharest and Cluj before travelling to Czechoslovakia. I
went along as an observer, not to play Boswell to his
Johnson, but because we both felt we would have a better
chance of talking undisturbed, away from the distractions of
home, where the demands of our careers and the ubiquitous
telephone might well make coherent conversation impossible.

Before our first talk, I tried to formulate some pattern
which would make the book acceptable, aware of the danger
that it could well turn out to be nothing more than a
shapeless mass of ill-connected thoughts, anecdotes and
observations. Lying in the bath (where all my most productive thinking is done), it seemed logical to divide our
lives into sections, and then to pursue the more general
ideas which would seem relevant to any particular period.
Thus, if we talked about adolescence, we could easily move

to a discussion of music in the lives of young people today; if we talked about personal experiences of working in film studios, we could progress to aesthetic considerations of the function of incidental music; if we exchanged personal experiences in the field of conducting (though I do not claim to even a fraction of his eminence in this), we would find an excuse to explore the more general aspects of this perennially fascinating subject.

Seated on a sofa in a Brussels hotel, with workmen noisily re-laying the marble tiled floor around us, we agreed on this plan as being the most practical and productive way of setting about a slightly daunting task; for it was our wish to air our thoughts on many topics, to talk easily and naturally as musicians do among themselves, and yet to produce something less transient than everyday conversation. After a preliminary chat lasting a bare half-hour, André, temporarily bearded, and looking like a sinister minor character from a Graham Greene film, was whisked away to join the orchestra on their charter flight to Rumania. "See you in Bucharest," he said, and then, characteristically added, "Hey, that's a pretty good exit line . . . " I was left alone to contemplate the prospect before me. I have always said that I could never write my own autobiography as I have such a hopeless memory for facts and, more particularly, the chronology of my life. Was this musical dialogue with a stranger going to be an indirect way of surveying my own past? Here were the threads of our two lives forcibly interwoven by a publisher's commission; I had long admired Previn for his versatility, but what right did I have to probe his mind? A ten-minute interview on a television programme is one thing; a joint book is a very different proposition. At that moment, the whole thing seemed to be a sort of literary gunshot wedding. I came to the conclusion that if the marriage was going to work, it must be on the basis of give-and-take—that I must contribute at least some share of my own, even though his star shines a good deal more brightly in the international sky than mine. In my determination not to become a sycophantic interviewer, I even comforted myself by assuming one small mantle of superiority; he was my junior by eight years. Why, if we had been at the same school, he would have been a scruffy little youngster when I was a senior prefect. Fortified by this specious argument, I made my way to the airport, walking an inch taller. That night, in Bucharest, our conversations began . . .

MUSIC FACE TO FACE

Antony Hopkins

It seems logical to begin with our childhoods, although mine was very uneventful musically. My father died when I was quite young, and I was adopted by a kind schoolmaster in Hertfordshire. A quiet, intensely reserved man, he didn't know a lot about music; he loved Gilbert and Sullivan, and church music. This was my musical diet for most of my formative years, apart from a number of piano rolls which I used to play on a pianola. I remember watching all those notes going down mechanically during the finale of Tchaikovsky's Fourth Symphony; I was fascinated by them, but I never heard the work on an orchestra until I was in my late 'teens. Music at an English public school in those days was not taken seriously, and I have never made up for the lack of technical foundation that came from having no real standard to work to when I was young. I realize now how valuable it would have been to have had more sense of competition; a musical child needs to have music going on around him. Certainly I could never have had anything like the fantastic keyboard facility you seem to have acquired when you were young.

André Previn

Well my musical background was that I was born in Berlin and my father was a quite successful lawyer and judge and he was a better than amateur pianist, much better in point of fact, and he was an amateur of music in the correct sense of that word. Some of my earliest recollections of life are hearing rather constant chamber music and visiting singers and instrumentalists with my father accompanying and playing away. And so I grew up in an atmosphere of music at all times and I am given to understand that I actually asked for lessons and got on rather well right away. My older brother and my older sister had already been taking lessons but under the pretext that all nice children take lessons ; but they weren't very interested and when I caught up with them within a few weeks, they were both filled with hatred and distress and quit. So then I was enrolled in the Conservatory very early on, as a child of six or seven and I studied with a man called Professor Brenhaupt and I remember mentioning that to George Szell many, many years later and he said, "Good Christ, he must have been eighty then", and of course to my recollection, I being six at the time, he seemed more like a hundred and twelve. I worked very hard but I always had what is known as a natural technique and had great facility. Even to this day if I don't practise I certainly know it, but I can get it back very quickly. That kind of skating on the surface technique, you know, not really deep technique. I enjoyed it a great deal and then when we left Germany to go to Paris I continued and then also in the States. So I had a really straightforward classically orientated Conservatory background with all the side lines, theory, harmony, counterpoint, the lot. And then we came to the United States where I continued with private teachers, with Joseph Achron and Ernst Toch and Mario Castelnuovo Tedesco. By that time it was a little away from actual piano learning, but rather I was much more keen on being a musician than a pianist and so I was always interested in the points of learning what to do with an orchestra and what the composition really consisted of and all that. My father was a book collector and he also had a lot of music; but I always wanted records which is a desire that is with me even to this moment. The first record I was ever given, which must have been I suppose when I was four, was an old ten-inch 78 r.p.m. record with a black label and gold lettering—of Stokowski and the Philadelphia orchestra doing "Fêtes" of Debussy and I played that with immense pleasure—to the point where really the old saying, that the records were worn through was quite true; and I remember what an extraordinary feeling of having completed some kind of circle it was for me when years later I recorded it.

A.H. Did you conduct when you were a child when you were listening to records?

A.P. I fervently hope not! I don't know, we had no home movies and I've not been told, mercifully.

A.H. Because practically the only classical recording that I was given—I think it was as late as my fifteenth birthday—was Beecham's performance of Beethoven's Second Symphony, and this was an absolute revelation to me. I used to play it over and over, but I loved to conduct it too. I remember that I had seen Stokowski's film *A Hundred Men and a Girl* which moved me profoundly. I fell deeply in love with Deanna Durbin, of course; but I remember watching Stokowski conducting and there was one moment during the Tchaikovsky Fifth Symphony when for some reason unknown to me this day, he raised four fingers towards the brass section. I don't know what he meant, but I felt this was a deeply significant gesture and I know that at any climax in this

3

	Beethoven symphony I always used to raise four fingers.
A.P.	Tomorrow's rehearsal will see me doing four fingers, that is marvellous.
A.H.	Talking about your family background being a musical one and the fact that your father was a better than average amateur pianist, did he play duets with you, because that's a marvellous way of being dragged along in the wake of a better pianist?
A.P.	That's how I learned most of the standard repertoire because I must say we banged through the nine Beethovens and most of the major Haydns, Mozarts and Schumanns in that way, and to this day I still see certain page-turns in my head. You know in the Pastorale I remember that one had a green cover and I remember there was a spot on page 4 at the primo part, you know—things like that, and that's never left me. When we came to the United States none of us knew one single syllable of English; my father could not afford to wait and learn the language in order to go back to law school so as to pass the Bar Exam to resume his practice, so he turned into a kind of neighbourhood piano teacher where the accent and the lack of language were an asset rather than a hindrance. They all adored being told in an accent what was wrong and he was damn good at it; and of course as always ... the music just continued in my house at every stage of my childhood and adolescence.
A.H.	I can remember just occasionally a man who was a proper pianist used to come and stay with us, and for a couple of days I would be really put through the mill. He used to read duets with me and I found this a very exhilarating experience. I can also remember the humiliation of being actually

4

locked into a room by him for the whole of an afternoon while I learned a piano transcription of some of the Schubert Rosamunde music. Later, I had an experience which I do think is worth recounting. I met a very musical family, who took to me, and invited me to go to Austria for a holiday. I was fifteen at the time and we went to a place called Schwaz. It was there, for the first time in my life, that I heard chamber music played superbly as a matter of course. It was a moment of revelation ; it was one of the turning-points in my life, and it was as a direct result of that that I was encouraged to take up music as a career, albeit still in a very limited way.

A.P.   When I was a child ... an adolescent ... I used to go to conductors' rehearsals and someone would come and do a piece which was not even necessarily profound but just complex, complex to beat, to rehearse, to figure out. And I used to sit there and in my heart of hearts I was convinced that I would never be able to do that, and I would go home in a private depression of great depth. And then years later when I had been rehearsing that same piece, it would suddenly strike me that that was indeed the piece that I thought I would never be able to do and here I hadn't given it a thought. If I see a student in the audience at a rehearsal of mine now, I wonder if he is undergoing the same unnecessary agony that we all go through.

A.H.   Do you ever get the feeling (which I have quite often) of "this can't be happening to me"? I mean have there been moments in your life when you've been conducting an orchestra, like the London Symphony, and you've suddenly realized that there you are, the same André Previn who once was a little boy in shorts, who once played the piano in the house in Berlin, and what are you doing up there for God's sake?

A.P.   Yes, but I think of it with the opposite of conceit. I think of it with trepidation. But I don't think of it while the music is going on, I think of it possibly in that endless second between the preparatory upbeat and the downbeat or when it's all over. But while it's going on, I must say it hasn't occurred to me.

A.H.   I'm thinking of how one stood as a student, watching the figures whom one idolized—a great pianist, great conductor, great violinist, whoever it might be. Suddenly you find yourself in that same position and in a way there's an emptiness about it because you don't get the satisfaction that you imagined that such a person must have.

A.P.   Well, I think you get it . . . I tend to romanticize and fantasize wildly anyway, and I had an experience last March which was very much like that : I had always resisted going back to Germany, and then they painted a very rosy picture of the concerts and I suddenly remembered that the first time I ever heard a live orchestra was when my father took me to the then public dress rehearsals of the Berlin Philharmonic with Furtwängler and I had heard the Brahms Fourth and the Academic Festival overture, and I suddenly realized that if I could programme those same works I would then go back. And I did do exactly that, and I went back (and I hadn't been in Berlin since I was a very small boy) and I went to try and look for the street where I was born. It had been bombed out pretty heavily and though I found the street with a driver, the house was gone and I was in an absolutely driving snowstorm. I walked round the street trying to find the tobacconist's where my father sent me for his

6

cigarettes or the laundry or whatever, and I suddenly remembered that there was a kiosk which used to advertise the Saturday—what in America we call the kiddie—matinée, and we would always go down and look at that kiosk and see if there was something playing at the movies on Saturday that we would be allowed to see. Well, I found the kiosk and just to determine whether that movie house was still in existence I went over and the placards were obliterated by the snow. And it was like a bad movie really, as much in life unfortunately seems to turn out to be . . . for I brushed the snow away with my hand and came upon my own name as conducting the Philharmonic that night. [Antony Hopkins: That's a *good* movie !] . . . It gave me the most extraordinary turn and that was a very important day for me.

A.H. You were talking about going to rehearsals as a youngster, something that happened to me in the years immediately before the war. I used to go from time to time, especially, I remember, to rehearsals with Beecham. There is one story which I think you will appreciate because it's a matter of conducting technique, particularly in rehearsals. Beecham came on to the platform at the beginning of a rehearsal and announced to the orchestra that they would start with Francesca da Rimini. He then began to talk quite quietly to the front desk of the violins, apparently about some matter of no great import. Now you know that this piece begins with the cellos and basses diving down to a low A flat. It's the sort of thing that an incompetent conductor might worry about a little, from the point of view of ensemble. I have never forgotten to this day the way in which Beecham coped with the problem ; as he

7

was talking to the violinists, he started to scratch the back of his neck with the baton in a very casual way. All the double-bass players were lying about on their instruments in that somnolent way that musicians have at the beginning of a morning's rehearsal, when suddenly, like one of the musketeers from Alexandre Dumas's immortal novel, Beecham flung the baton towards them, just like a rapier thrust. I have never heard such an attack. They were totally unready for it, but the moment that the gesture came, they flung themselves at their instruments and this immensely exciting sound cut into the silence of the hall. I would love to have known whether he did the same trick at the concert, or whether he gave them a proper upbeat!

A.P. That's a lovely story. I think those things have a tendency to happen at rehearsals because there isn't any way to have the players unprepared at an actual concert, you know. The anticipatory silence makes one nervous and prevents somebody from taking the kind of gamble and starting in that way. What I am trying to say is that suppose it had resulted in chaos it wouldn't have mattered. And nobody is going to gamble like that in a concert—which is in a way too bad too.

A.H. There's a nice story about one of the players getting his own back on Beecham. You know he was an absolute sadist about the start of Weber's Overture to Oberon, where the horn has to play those three very quiet notes. Alan Civil, who is one of the great horn players in the world today, told me that time and again, Beecham kept him waiting in a state of expectant frenzy to play these three notes while he cleaned his glasses, looked at the audience, fiddled with the score, did anything possible to put off the evil moment when

8

the player actually had to begin. At one of the very last concerts that Beecham ever conducted, he came doddering on and acknowledged the tremendous reception of the audience; as he turned round, Alan Civil started to play the overture all on his own, and he said he never saw a conductor pick up a baton so quickly in his life!

A.P.   It's a good Beecham story, it's a typical Alan Civil story . . . yes, that's first rate. Did you ever get to put pencil to paper when you were a child?

A.H.   Well, in my very early piano lessons, which were given to me by a splendid lady called Miss Hedges, I used to have a reward. If I had worked well that week she would write down for me a piece that I composed, and I still have to this day an album of pieces which I wrote . . .

A.P.   At what age was this?

A.H.   This was at seven; indeed, the one positive contribution which my adoptive mother made towards my musical education was that she did encourage me from about the age of five to play little descriptive pieces on the piano out of my head. I was also a prodigious reader as a child. I could read fluently when I went to kindergarten. When other children were dealing with "The cat sat on the mat" I used to be put in a corner to read *The Listener*—I was that much ahead of them.

A.P.   There seems to be a small extra musical thing that we have in common because I read very early on, and one of my father's favourite sports was to tell visitors—I am given to understand again—that I could read fluently, and when doubt was expressed he would hand me a volume of Gibbon and have me read from it; of course I read like a parrot, without understanding, but my father was so pleased! After we came to this country we were

9

in dire straits financially; but when it came to expenditure of money on books, he allowed as free a hand as it was possible for us to have, and I never lacked for books. And I even went to work in the neighbourhood bookstore, kind of sweeping up, cleaning up at no money but for books. That doesn't seem to be very prevalent any more. Did you ever have anything to do with youth orchestras when you were a child? When I was a child in California there was a very remarkable man called Peter Meremblum, and he founded something called the California Youth Symphony, and this orchestra became quite famous. There was one for the really little kids and one for, let's say, up to eighteen. They rehearsed every Saturday morning and it got to the point where every big conductor who came to Los Angeles would come and rehearse them, and that was the whole idea. Peter Meremblum was I think more dedicated as an educator than he was accomplished as a conductor, but he did make it a point to have ... I mean the damndest people would show up, you know—Rodzinski and Mitropoulos and anybody who was there, and I was kind of a standby piano soloist and I did my very first downbeat with them. I'll tell you something funny; Peter Meremblum was very Russian and of a certain kind of Russian musical persuasion, and so these kids were not terribly good at playing the most standard symphonic literature, let's say Brahms First for instance; but they played the Glazunov Fifth Symphony and obscure Tchaikovsky overtures, and I remember it was the first time I ever heard Glinka other than *Ruslan and Ludmila*, and endless other strange pieces of which to this day I can't find the scores. I learned them there in a haphazard way and that was my first exposure

	to youth orchestras, and it stood me in good stead because that is why I like to work with them now as you do.
A.H.	Did you ever compete in the big national or international competitions that are such a feature of musical life nowadays?
A.P.	Well, I entered three competitions and I came second in all three so I thought that was my role in life for a while; but I did have some of the oddest first jobs—I mean for money—as a player. As I said, when we came to the United States we were really stuck for money.
A.H.	I take it as a family you were all talking German at this stage.
A.P.	Oh yes. I was simply thrown into public school, into grammar school in the United States without knowing one single word—which was both cruel and practical, because I learnt it very fast, very slangy and with not too many cares about it. You know, instead of ... if I had been put through the torture of a tutor at home I would have been careful of what I was saying, but it would probably have taken me a lot longer ...
A.H.	I suppose you continued to talk German at home, although you had to talk English or American at school ... ?
A.P.	Yes, I grew up totally bilingual. But the first job I had was really very odd. In downtown Los Angeles there was a department store called Barker Brothers, I suppose like Harrods except not nearly so grand. On the sixth floor they had electric organs and at age ... twelve or thirteen, I would go there after school from four to six till closing and sit there playing that kind of meaningless drivel which I suppose is played on electric organs at home, kind of *By a Waterfall* ... those things.

A.H.   *The Star Folio of Classical Gems . . .*
A.P.   Yes, right, *Music the Whole World Loves*. I would sit and plough through this nonsense and get $1·50 for the two hours and that would see me through the week for lunches and other extravagances. Then I got a job playing the piano in a cinema which re-ran silent films only. It was my first crack at improvising, since I was never given the opportunity of looking at the films beforehand. It was also the first time I was ever sacked. Here's how that happened : I was improvising a score to the great classic D. W. Griffith epic *Intolerance*. This film kept jumping backwards and forwards in time, from biblical days to the Roaring Twenties, and it was a very dodgy business for me to be spot on with the correct atmospheric music. At any rate, at one point I thought they had settled into a nice long sequence of Charleston-dancing flappers, and I swung wholeheartedly into *Tiger Rag*. The next thing I saw was the manager, apoplectic, storming down the centre aisle. I threw a quick glance at the screen and realized that I had been doing my best Fats Waller imitation to the Crucifixion. No one seemed to appreciate the inadvertent black humour and I was summarily dismissed. They used records for the rest of the day.

A.H.   I suppose nowadays it would be regarded as being a very "in" thing to have the Crucifixion accompanied by a music track playing *Tiger Rag!*
A.P.   Absolutely . . .

A.H.   There's one point I haven't touched on at all with regard to this period of your adolescence. When you arrived in America, unable to speak a word of English, and with a father who was devoted to what we call serious music, one would expect you to have continued evolving in that direction. In fact, it seemed that you had an extraordinary natural gift for playing jazz. Now was this simply the result of the American environment, and what did your parents say when they found you doing this?

A.P. I was, as any adolescent is, interested in the pop music of the day, which was not what you call pop music now, but which was either dance bands (which I didn't care for very much) or jazz, which I did like. I was always interested in improvisation and I used to improvise on anything . . . on any given theme; I mean even when I was a very, very small child I would sit down and play awful variations on, say, *Santa Lucia* for hours to the distress of everybody. The element of improvisation has I think unfortunately gone out of classical music to a great extent. One of my teachers in Paris, Marcel Dupré, was the last extraordinary exponent of that. He can sit down and upon given notes improvise an absolute strict four or five voice fugue on the organ which was enough to baffle everybody.

A.H. But it's a talent that only organists develop among serious musicians today . . .

A.P. Well, I used to think it was because you couldn't tell really what the hell was going on anyway, but with Dupré you could and it was incredible. But anyway what happened was that I was interested in jazz, but no more than very casually. Then someone gave me an album of 78 r.p.m. records by a pianist called Art Tatum. [Antony Hopkins : He was blind wasn't he?] Yes, he was blind. And he was a jazz pianist whom Horowitz admired very much. And it was the first time that I had ever heard someone get that inventive harmonically, rhythmically and whatever-else-

13

have-you within the 32-bar structure of a pop song. It was the first time I heard anyone negate the basic value of that 32-bar song that much in favour of the improvisatory element and it was also the first time that I had ever heard a jazz pianist use the piano to its fullest extent. He was very much a solo pianist; he was not at all interested in playing with a group and so what I did was typically German I suppose, or typically classical: I sat like an absolute fool and wrote out all those elaborate solos on his records. I don't know if you've heard them—but he used to play at blinding speeds with absolutely endless cascading runs, and the fact that I would sit and copy them out was really one of the labours of Sisyphus, wasn't it?

A.H. It's a very good example of practical aural training at a higher level all the same.

A.P. Possibly, but it would have done me a damn sight more good if I had copied out scores of Mozart's. But anyway there it is. So for years I played a kind of fifth-grade imitation Art Tatum for many reasons, though mainly because it suited my technique. I got a great kick out of it. And when it got to the point where I was able to use my own mind I became a very bad second-rate jazz pianist. Nevertheless, I was very young and I was able to make a few dollars at it. And then came the absolutely crassest reason of all and that is that we were very broke. I was not the recipient of an allowance per week, and I was interested in buying some records and music. So I was able to put together some money by playing at dancing schools, with a drummer and a bass player, at private dances, anywhere. Out of that I met musicians much better than myself and I grew to have certain idols as pianists and this went on and on. And when I was about sixteen, I made an album of jazz piano for RCA which is now luckily out of print; but a strange thing happened which is either fortunate or unfortunate, depending on the point of view, and that is that it was an absolutely runaway success and sold something like 200,000 copies and of course out of that came another album.

A.H.   Would this be partly because you were sixteen or because it was remarkable jazz playing?

A.P.   I don't know. It didn't have my picture on the cover and it didn't say very much about me, so I like to think that it wasn't totally due to the fact that I was that young, besides which in jazz you don't have the prodigy element and nobody really cares about age. At any rate, I made another album which was not a success but the first one was still going strong so I made still another one. It's kind of funny, I chased the success of that first one for about ten years and I only hit it about twice more. But anyway, I was suddenly in the curious position of having a commodity at my finger-tips which made money...

A.H.   More than the $1·50 you had been collecting on the organ...

A.P.   Yes, and I couldn't resist it and frankly, without making apologies for it, I don't know of a lot of sixteen-year-olds that would. And what has happened since is that some of these albums exist in the minds of people with flatteringly long memories, and they started thinking of me as a jazz performer whereas in reality I was always just a musician who enjoyed playing jazz.

A.H.   What was your father's reaction to this? Was he stuffy about it? Did he think you were betraying your art or anything like that?

A.P.   I wonder. He may have done so in his innermost

thoughts. He did not voice it. He was very, very good and fair about it since it didn't involve practising. I am sure that if I had had rehearsals with groups at our house, he would have hated it; but it's not the kind of music you sit and practise a lot at home. I don't think he ever heard the difference between styles. I know for a fact that Horowitz once heard two totally different tunes played by Art Tatum and he genuinely thought it had been the same song—which is an incredible admission to me because he couldn't hear the harmonic elements at all. My father was really old-style and Germanic and all that and his favourite criticism of any piece of music, jazz or serious or otherwise, was "Well it's not the *Eroica*" —and it was pointless to say that it was never meant to be the *Eroica* and everything must not be measured against the *Eroica*. I enjoyed not only the musical side of jazz but I enjoyed the camaraderie which was extraordinarily warm and generous. There was very little of the jockeying for position that the good students at a Conservatory have and I made some lifelong lasting friends. The attitude of the jazz musician is quite admirable and I mean under really insanely adverse conditions; they don't have the tendency to get as depressed by externals as . . . well, as I do now in point of fact or as the men in a symphony orchestra do, because the jazz musicians feel that everything that matters is in the music that night. It may have something to do with the fact that it is not prepared, it's not scholarly, it's not studied. It really just comes out of that one person's head.

A.H.   Do you think it's because it just happens that one time, whereas if you've got to play a Beethoven symphony you're still playing the same

16

notes, and always trying to find a little something more in them?

A.P.   Yes. You see, that's the main argument I have against people who hope to combine the two, quite apart from other arguments which we might go into later. The whole point of jazz is to have music of the absolute moment, that instant, ephemeral and fleeting; that is the idea, that is the thing you go for. The whole idea is never to repeat anything, and therefore it is not music meant to be *kept* anywhere, whereas— the idea of all serious music is to have it as permanent as possible. So the two have a completely different outlook, a whole different responsibility to begin with, and therefore I think the efforts to combine them are both musically fruitless and philosophically hopeless.

A.H.   Were you pursuing what you might call a self-study course in serious music at the same time, playing Beethoven at home, and playing things like *Summertime* at night?

A.P.   Constantly, and not only at home. I was also doing concerts. This is where retrospectively I have great regrets. I was at that time making my living working at film studios as an orchestrator at first, arranger, and then composer, and I was fitting my concerts into my film schedule, and that of course was unforgivable.

A.H.   Were you still in your teens then, while working in those film studios?

A.P.   Yes, I went to work as an orchestrator at MGM when I was sixteen.

A.H.   How did you convince them that you could do it?

A.P.   Well, it was a different world then for the films. Let's see, when I was sixteen it was 1946. At that time there were endless movies being made, as many as there are TV shows now. Everything was a success. MGM was the biggest studio in the world at that time and they made musical after musical after musical. There was a period of about five years when Esther Williams never dried off and of course every time she jumped in there had to be two harps minimum . . . and they simply ran out of people who could write for that or who were willing to write for that . . .

A.H. . . . so that you jumped in at the bottom of the pool . . .

A.P. Well, exactly, and the waters closed round me! Do you remember that in those days José Iturbi had ambitions to be a film star?

A.H. I saw all those movies in London, the glass piano and everything.

A.P. And he never took his pipe out of his mouth even while he was playing the *Appassionata*. He was a very nice man and the studio thought that he should play some jazz. Not really jazz, but some jazz-tinged things and of course, he had no idea how to do that. But I was told later that the studio heard vague rumours about this obnoxious kid, namely me, who could play jazz and who was classically-trained and therefore could conceivably write out these improvisatory sounding things, so I did do that for Iturbi and he enjoyed it. And then they said well, now, an orchestra should accompany this, so go and show these piano things to Mr. X and he will write an orchestration. And I said well, I would just as soon do it myself, and they let me. So after that I did anything I was asked to, and that is how I was at the studios. But at the same time the jazz was always a side line and I played an immense amount of chamber music in those days. I'll tell you a nice thing about when I first started to play chamber music. There are very, very few things that I am pleased with myself about musically, and I mean that very deeply ; but I am a good sight-reader. I can sight-read just about anything, unless it's by Xenakis in which case my mathematics don't suffice. We had a principal cellist in the MGM orchestra at that time called Willem Vandenberg who was also the associate conductor of the LA Philharmonic for a while. He was a great friend of Joseph Szigeti's. Szigeti lived in a Los Angeles suburb called Palos Verdes and he was looking for someone to play trios. This Willy Vandenberg said to him, "We have a young man"—I was, I guess, sixteen or seventeen—"who can sight-read anything." Szigeti, who was a great champion of modern music, used to have reams of music sent to him ; much of it was still in manuscript. Vandenberg took me up to Szigeti's house and all this stuff was put in front of me. But don't forget in those days it was still written on standard music paper, which made things a lot easier. And I struggled through pages of it, and Szigeti, after a particularly rough session, said, "Let's relax and play a Beethoven trio, the three of us." "André," he said, "what would you like to play, which one ?" And I said—this is very much like you, Tony, because you said you had hardly heard a Beethoven symphony at the age of seventeen—I said, "Well, I've never played any," and there was a pause during which you could have played Bruckner Eight, and then Szigeti, looking at me the way one looks at a rare specimen under a microscope, said, "What do you mean, you've never played any of the Beethoven trios ?" and I said, "I just never have." And he did something for which I will never forget him, it was so kind and generous and thoughtful.

He started with Trio Number One and he said to me, "You will now come back every Monday and I will give you supper and we will play for two hours, and we will have some coffee or a drink and we will play for two hours more, and we're going to play all the Beethovens, all the Brahms, all the Schuberts, all the Mozarts until you know what chamber music is about. You're a very good pianist and it is absolutely bloody disgraceful." And I went back for months, every Monday night. My introduction to chamber music was through Szigeti and what he did not know about Beethoven trios was truly not worth knowing. It was extremely generous, and I grew to love chamber music even more. I was playing as soloist in an occasional concerto from time to time but I did waste a lot of years playing and conducting only occasionally and sporadically, and being at the studio. But you see, again, it's very difficult to be sixteen to seventeen and making a very comfortable living at MGM . . . after all, I bought a sports-car and met chorus girls, you know, it was Utopia . . . what did I want with learning scores? I guess I had to go through that.

A.H.   There's one little story here I ought to tell you, because it's something that I would like to be remembered about him. You mentioned Horowitz several times. My great god among pianists was Rachmaninoff. [André Previn: Well, naturally.] I was told by a friend of mine that she was in a night-club in New York one night and at about three o'clock, the band decided they had had enough and went home. The place was practically deserted when suddenly she heard from the piano the most marvellous sweet jazz, played with wonderful luxuriant richness of harmony. The very few customers that remained became abso-

20

lutely hushed as they listened to this; they realized it was someone quite exceptional. Only when she went over to have a look to see who was playing, did she realize it was Rachmaninoff. [André Previn: It was *Rachmaninoff*?] Yes, and he just sat down at the piano and played for his own pleasure.

A.P. I find that absolutely extraordinary because I would have thought that his whole approach to music was anti-strict tempo.

A.H. Yes, well when I say "sweet jazz" I mean that he was presumably playing things like Gershwin. If you can imagine a Rachmaninoff transcription of *Summertime*, well that's what they got.

A.P. Good God, what a seductive idea. Well, for instance, Ashkenazy is fascinated by jazz and feels that he could play it, and I don't doubt that he could. Sometimes he and I will sit down and see what we can do, because he loves to improvise and he has a pixie sense of improvisation anyway, and it would be very amusing and nice if he could . . . if it gave him pleasure of course.

A.H. What you've been describing not only fills me with an envy which is more green than I like to say, but also leads very conveniently on to what I feel is a general issue which I do think we should discuss at this point. It's the whole question of education, because a little question-mark rose out of my mind as you talked to me about what you were doing at sixteen and seventeen. The fact is that in England you just wouldn't have been allowed to do it, because you would have to have been at school, complying with the requirements of the Ministry of Education.

A.P. I did that in America too.

A.H. So you were doing all this but you were also doing schoolwork?

A.P.   Oh yes. I didn't really do anything as glamorous as skipping school to go and play with my jazz friends. No, no,—I was leading a very straightforward life.

A.H.   But also orchestrating for MGM and going to Szigeti for chamber music?

A.P.   Yes, there was something almost farcical about it. I used to get through with school at 3.30, jump on a bus still carrying the geometry books, show up at MGM and go down to a rehearsal hall and watch a dance routine, take it down and then go home, start work on the necessary music for it, go on to my school homework. You know, I did enjoy it all. I'm kind of sorry that energy flags in later years. I couldn't keep up that schedule of my youth for more than a week now without totally collapsing.

A.H.   Anyway, can we get back to this question of musical education because you see, in my own case, I really was not seriously taught anything about music until I was very nearly twenty. From the age of sixteen I did have a teacher who made me think about wider musical issues. He would let me see books which showed me the sort of environment in which Mozart lived; he made me think quite deeply about historical issues, not in their small or narrow sense, but in their widest musical implications. For this, I am very grateful; but what I needed was a stern disciplinarian of a piano teacher who would make me buckle down and just do technique. Meantime, there I was in an English public school—in a pretty philistine atmosphere, not being exposed to much music at all. I went to the occasional concert for young people, such as the Malcolm Sargent youth concerts. I went once to a Promenade Concert when I was about seventeen and heard Cyril

Smith play the Rachmaninoff Third. That was another critical turning-point in my life because I wrote such an idolizing fan letter that he still remembered it three years later when I bumped into him on the staircase at the Royal College. The result was that I became his pupil for a year and a half, and he helped me a lot. But he still didn't help me as much as a good teacher would have done much earlier on, because by the time you're twenty, you know, you're old and arthritic as far as piano playing is concerned unless you've got the nervous and muscular foundations right. [André Previn: Like tennis champions.] Yes. What I think we should discuss now, as far as the differing environments which we both experienced, is in what ways do you think one ought to cope with the problem of a really musically talented child? If one subjects them to the ordinary drill of a conventional education, you don't give them time to develop those physical aspects of musicianship which are really the equivalent of what a ballet dancer has to do, when the bones are still supple.

A.P. Well, yes we can discuss that. I am also very interested in discussing the musical education of the not specifically talented child.

A.H. Yes, but could we start with the talented ones because we're starting with you and to a lesser extent with me.

A.P. But don't you see that neither one of us did badly. I mean, I think this may sound—do you have the term "Pollyanna" in England? [Antony Hopkins: I don't think so, no, I don't know how to spell it even!] Well, it's after a nauseating children's story about a little girl who saw the good side of absolutely everything, you know in the middle of World War II she would have found something

23

marvellous. Well, anyway it seems to me that I have to be Pollyanna on this subject. I have never encountered anyone with a definite talent who didn't eventually make it.

A.H.   I think I would agree with you there. I distrust the attitude that says, "I am a great genius and the world doesn't take any notice of me."

A.P.   Of course it is undeniable that there are many unknown artists who are more gifted than their famous counterparts, and that is shameful and unfair. I have often felt personal guilt when I see how many vastly talented people there are still trying to get their first break. Nevertheless, if someone is a wonderfully gifted performer or creator, I am convinced that eventually he will make himself heard. But in terms of education I am not a great believer in a scholarly education for musicians. I am a great believer in the most practical side of it. I think if you are a composer then you must compose for any group that is available, amateur, semi-professional, professional; if the only three friends you have play tuba, mouth-organ and bicycle pump, then write something for those three things and hear it.

A.H.   I agree a hundred per cent with that.

A.P.   I went through both kinds of education. Let's say that a teacher whom you idolized at Conservatory corrected a student score of yours and told you, "This won't sound good because..." and then listed fifteen excellent and learned reasons. Well, that kind of abstract lesson is much harder to assimilate than actually hearing the mistake. When I was given an assignment at MGM on a Monday, I always had the assurance that I would hear my music played by the very best professionals within the week. I would sit on the scoring stage, dead tired, ticking off

24

	moments in my score and telling myself "No, that's awful, yes, that's all right, no, never do that again" and so on.
A.H.	I know this experience myself. I think this is one of the great values of writing incidental music.
A.P.	On the other hand I find that there is at the moment a great idolatory of the primitive and I have never been interested in that. There is a trend in criticism now to say "he has too much technique". I don't think it is possible to have too much technique. I simply don't. As a composer, as an interpreter, as anything.
A.H.	What they really mean is that he is flaunting his technique.
A.P.	Yes, but a favourite gambit these days seems to be : "He plays all the notes but I would rather hear the intent of the music." Well, I personally would rather hear both. And conversely, a much-loved phrase one can hear around the Festival Hall bar at any concert interval is, "Of course he misses a lot of the notes, but my god, the musicianship, the sincerity !" It would seem to me, at the risk of sounding churlish, that the composer wrote down all those notes because he wanted to hear them all played. To get back to your original question ; for a talented child the most important aspect of his musical education is the absolute beginning. Too many talents have been thrown away because of the efforts of a martinet teacher or the zeal of an over-ambitious mother. Too many hours of practice too early in life will truly prevent a real flowering of love for music. It is infinitely better for a child to grow up committed to music, and loving it, and reacting to it and needing it, than to be put off by disciplinarian tactics.
A.H.	Yes ; may I pin you down a little more specifically

on this by quoting a few examples? You see, there are a number of people about in the world today, like Yehudi Menuhin, who did not have a normal childhood since they had embarked on the career of child virtuoso. They had a childhood which, from the conventional point of view, lacked the ordinary educational curriculum; and yet these people are highly articulate, really intelligent, and educated in the widest sense of the word. Most of them speak four or five languages which they have picked up in the course of travelling around; the lack of a conservative, formal type of education certainly hasn't done them any harm. Well, now if we go to a slightly lower level than that, I would like to quote a specific instance to you. I was adjudicating, some years ago, at a music festival at Harrogate, and in the evening they had a class for "Violin Concerto, Open". I had listened to about five rather indifferent performances by adults when the final entry of the class came on the stage. I looked up and saw a small girl aged eleven, in a gym slip, looking like a poster for Oxfam. She had a little white face with great dark eyes and very thin pipe-stem legs, and she stood there with a violin beside her. I saw she was down to play the Mozart A Major Concerto, and my heart sank and I thought, "Oh God must I have this at this time of the day!" She then played, and within six notes I knew that I was hearing somebody who knew how to phrase, who had a wonderful natural sense of musicianship, and who could play the violin. Instead of writing a report on this, saying that the first phrase was beautiful, and what a pity the C sharp on page 27 was out of tune or something, I wrote an impassioned letter to her headmistress and said, "Dear head-

26

mistress : I don't know who you are, and forgive me for writing to you in this way but this child has such a talent that you should turn a blind eye to every requirement of the Ministry of Education, and give her an opportunity to practise at least three hours every day without pressure. By all means carry on with the normal curriculum of education as far as you must, but to deprive her of the opportunity of developing this talent would be to kill something which really is of the very first quality." Well, in fact the parents took the girl away from school when she was about fifteen and sent her to study with Endré Wolf, and when she was eighteen she won the BBC Concerto Prize. It was Maureen Smith. Now her mother has told me that many times they wondered if they were right in doing this ; should they play safe by giving her a general education so that, she could always fall back on teaching if necessary? But because I had been so emphatic about this, they stuck it out and they said, "Right, we believe in this child now and we're going to give her this chance." I believe that unless she had been taken away from school, unless they had taken her to a first-class teacher, then this mightn't have happened the same way.

A.P.   Yes, you're quite right. If she were really an absolute amazing talent then I like to think that she would have somehow still triumphed because she would have made the time. [Antony Hopkins : Why should she have to make the time? It should be given to her.] Well, of course it should be given to her. One of the most lethal things a parent can do to a child who shows an early proclivity to an instrument, is instantly to convince him—no, threaten him—that he is going to be the future Rubinstein or Isaac Stern or Segovia or Rostropovich. From that moment on, the poor child is fighting for his life. Why is it always deemed necessary for every gifted youngster to go on to being a professional musician? I can think of no lovelier gift than to be able to play an instrument well enough to give oneself pleasure and relaxation, well enough to appreciate great playing by others, well enough to be an initiate into the mysteries of music. None of these automatically mean competing with every virtuoso alive!

A.H.   I'm not contesting that as a general viewpoint at all, and I was rather pinning you down on a particular example. I don't think anybody would quarrel with what you've just been saying, and there is a long-overdue trend now in Engand to start specialized schools for children who are musically endowed. But personally, I cannot conceive why it is more important in a subject like history to learn about battles and politics than it is to learn about the way musicians lived. If you're going to teach history to a musical child, why not learn about the nineteenth century mainly through the environment of Schubert and Beethoven, rather than through other historical figures? After all they are part of history.

A.P.   And I would think a damned sight more important than all the people who seem to have won battles. I've been harbouring a dream situation in terms of a normal generalized education; any normal schooling anywhere in the world includes basic arithmetic, right? If you take to it, if you have a flair for it, then you may go on to mathematics, algebra, trigonometry, calculus, on and on. Well, suppose that the most rudimentary musical education—just the reading of treble and bass clef—were just as compulsory as arithmetic. Those that liked it, could pursue it on to higher planes, but even those who would call it a day after the basic year would have had a door opened to them that is more valuable than a great many of the facts which are stuffed into one at school and which one never uses again. Such an education would lead to so many progressions : first of all, it would lead to what I call active rather than passive listening, for the simple reason that the basic mystery of music would already have been solved long ago. Don't forget that music is written down in what must seem like hieroglyphics to most people, decipherable by only a very select few. It is a very private form of art, and, unlike painting, where creation and performance are simultaneous, always needs the performing middle man.

A.H.　This is actually happening I think to a greater degree than you may realize. In practically every school in the country, children are given some musical experience, particularly of course through all the recent emphasis on work with pentatonic percussion instruments.

A.P.　But that's wonderful ; you see I am too recent a resident of England to have known that. Just to carry it to what might seem a ludicrous extreme, if you can read music, the chances are you will practise some kind of music in the home. If you practise some kind of music in the home and play badly, it will always lead you to wanting to hear that instrument played well ; ergo, you would go to hear someone play it well, and thereby be exposed to more music. Another thing is that composers would suddenly find it necessary, through the request of their publishers if nothing else, to provide some music for those people to play in the home. And you would suddenly have a great call for simple music, and you would have

	a real renaissance of amateur music which I think is more valuable to the future of music than the highest level of professionalism.
A.H.	This raises a whole host of issues in my mind which I feel strongly about, if we can grapple with them now. I'd like to tell you what Jacqueline Dupré's mother did at her school. She used to teach music in a large grammar school in Hemel Hempstead and she got the children, all of them under twelve, to write an opera. It took an hour to perform and was based on a Russian legend; the libretto was written by a member of the English staff, and the kids were allotted sections of this work. They wrote the music and, of course, to a critical ear it was certainly quite crude in many ways. The harmony was a bit thin in places, and there were all sorts of "musico-grammatical" errors of one kind or another.
A.P.	How young was the youngest?
A.H.	I would think about nine. It was scored for an orchestra of about twenty-five to thirty players provided from the school-children.
A.P.	Who scored it?
A.H.	Oh, the kids themselves. That was the point. The whole thing was done with the absolute minimum of interference from the teachers; the children found out by experiment what came off and what didn't. They would listen to a passage and decide it was a bit thin; so they would thicken it up, usually by adding a bit more percussion. But the result, to my mind, was a marvellous instance of creative music at a rather more ambitious level than is usually attempted with children of that age, and certainly their involvement was terrific. But it was the comment that Iris Dupré made at the end of this which really brought despair into my heart, and this is what I want to discuss with

30

you now. Because as she said, the tragedy was that she then had to undo all this work by teaching the children the examination syllabus requirements for "O" level music. This is something I feel passionately about, that exams in music are a complete travesty; if they must exist, they are orientated in completely the wrong direction. Now what do you feel about this?

A.P.   I feel the same as you. I talked to a young conductor who was the winner of the Mitropoulos prize and there was an examination just to enter the competition itself. The young man showed me what the entrance requirements were—this was a few months ago, and I'll be totally open with you, I couldn't enter that exam now, and I doubt whether a hell of a lot of my colleagues could, because it required knowledge that . . . well, it required knowledge that I wish I had, but also that I would not use in my work with my orchestra over a period of unforeseeable years. In exams, they often mistake information for knowledge. To this day I don't know the Koechel numbers, in Mozart, I don't know opus numbers and I couldn't at this moment tell you the date of Bizet's birthday, but on the other hand, I know all the music from *Carmen*.

A.H.   But if I take a specific instance, I think you will agree with me that the Mozart letters are some of the most extraordinarily vivid pictures of a historical period which you could possibly find. Not only that, but when one reads them, Mozart comes alive as a human being in such a way as to affect one's entire concept of how to interpret his music, or even of just how to listen to it. Now let's assume for the moment that some enlightened examiner decides, because he thinks it's a good thing to read the Mozart letters, to make them the set book for an examination in musical history; it is my hunch that the exam questions would be based not on the content of the letters at all, but the content of the footnotes. To the examining mind, the footnote is more important than the letter because the footnote shows a sort of scholastic respectability.

A.P.   It's a great game because you could take a letter about how he was on a pilgrimage to see Haydn, for instance. And the question probably would be "How long was the coach ride?"

A.H.   I've talked a lot at teachers' conferences about this, and I remember on one occasion, I was actually asked to try to prepare an examination syllabus for a Music exam. Do you know, every single constructive suggestion that I made was blocked because it didn't have the answer "Yes" or "No". The teachers said "We must have an answer which is right or wrong—yes or no". Why? Because music isn't like that: it isn't hard and fast. One can hear six different performances of the Emperor Concerto and all of them can be right in their own particular way.

A.P.   Yes; I mean there is room for interpretation not only in the actual making of music but in the attitude about music.

A.H.   But how can one reconcile this with the requirements of an examination syllabus? Is the answer to throw the exams out of the window?

A.P.   I would think so, yes, surely.

A.H.   But then if you do that, what sort of filter do you have?

A.P.   I think that the filter is natural, Tony. Let me cite an example: My wife's sister's husband is a young painter and whatever he knows about painting, about the history of painting, he has picked up through the love of it. Yet if he were to take an exam to enter an art institute, I am sure he would fail. At the same time his talent and his ambition is so inborn that he will become an important painter, and I have no doubt about that. And if I, at almost any point in my life, had been told that "if you fail this exam you will not be allowed to become a musician," I would now be, I don't know, a plumber somewhere.

A.H. Look, André, I'm in business as a popular educator. The thing I am best known for is broadcasting about music, and time and again people write to me or say to me in conversation, "You are such a musical scholar." This always arouses an indignant reaction on my part. I say I am *not* a scholar, because I am not, in any sense of the word. If, when I am writing a script about a Beethoven quartet or sonata or whatever it may be, I want a specific fact about what year it was written, I simply go and look it up in a book, because that's what books are for. I even believe that in the process of absorbing a great deal of factual information in an ordinary university course of four years, one can lose something of the immediacy of impact, of the quality that inspires a passionate involvement with music. Perhaps the reason why I can communicate with a radio public is because so often the music is a fresh experience for me as well, at that moment in my life. I very often broadcast about things I've never heard before and so I hear them as it were with washed ears. I hear them without prejudging what they're going to sound like, without having a preconception which has been drilled into me by somebody else. Consequently, when I listen to the music, I listen to it with a mature musical mind but without prior knowledge. This seems to me to be something which is surely worth treasuring.

A.P.   There's been much too much noise made about certain "holy" names which simply must not be criticized. It's wonderful to hear music with new ears, it enables one to cut right through that whole emperor's-new-clothes syndrome. Some university students heard a new piece by a very very avant-garde composer; the work had already received write-ups which demanded your being a Rhodes scholar just to get through the vocabulary of the review, not to mention the music of the work itself. But, of course, the students didn't know that, and it was the general consensus of opinion that they had heard, if I may quote verbatim, "a load of crap". I grant you that Bernard Shaw chose his scathing words more beautifully, but nevertheless, the point was made loud and clear. Do you know Oliver Knussen, the young English composer? He is now eighteen years old and incredibly talented. He has written several symphonies, concertos, song cycles and chamber music. He finds Beethoven almost unbelievably boring. Now it would be terribly harmful to tell him flatly "you're wrong". Anyone as gifted as he will eventually come round to discovering at least certain Beethoven that would speak to him of a human experience which he is at the moment too young to have known. Vaughan Williams in a marvellous essay of his said he knows the Ninth Symphony is a masterpiece beyond any doubt but it is written in a language the vocabulary of which he does not like.

A.H.   I would say that about some of the Vaughan Williams symphonies.

A.P.   At any rate I think it's very dangerous to say to a child "this is Mozart so you must love it; this is Bach so you must admire it."

A.H.   Is it possible that you and I are witnessing the

34

emergence of a generation to whom the language of the nineteenth and the eighteenth century is in fact so far removed that they will never become completely identified with it?

A.P.   No, I tend to doubt that. I doubt that simply because before e. e. cummings went on into a world of small letters, he did learn what the English language was; and before someone like Fontana decided to slash a canvas, he did go and look at Velazquez. I don't think it will be possible for a young composer to disregard all precedent. I've never met one who is willing to, only the fakes; and one thing that worries me about myself so much, and where I feel a great lack of knowledge, is that when it comes to the absolute last word in experimental music I find myself very hard put to recognize the truly significant from the total fraud at first hearing. I really mean that, not for the sake of a wisecrack. If someone very clever were to sit down and send me up with an improvisation, and then I heard a new piece by, let's say, Stockhausen, I am not sure I would know which was the fake. I am sure it's my loss more than anything else, but it is also a rather sad commentary because I am a professional, and I would know in the normal course of musical language which was the fake and which wasn't. I get a great many scores sent to me every single week, and as a conductor I have my own private rule—it might sound facetious, but it's true: if I find the explanatory footnotes on what all the symbols mean in the music are longer than the piece itself, I will not conduct it.

A.H.   Can we finish this whole question of the young and music with a few things which we haven't touched on? You did say, when you were a boy in California, you played in an orchestra which you felt

35

was something of a landmark in musical life there at the time ... [André Previn : Oh yes.] Well, that's no longer a rarity ; in this country, practically every county has a youth orchestra and, of course, we have a National Youth Orchestra. It is not unique to us ; they have Jeunesses Musicales in France, in Canada, astonishing student orchestras in Japan, and so on. Now, do you think that although this is obviously a tremendous ideal from the point of view of involving young people, are we in a sense betraying them by leading them to believe that there's going to be room for them all in the musical profession—because frankly there isn't going to be, is there?

A.P.   No, I don't think that everyone who sits in the Leicestershire School Orchestra thinks he is going to play in the LSO ; but it doesn't do any harm to hope for it and again it just leads back to reiterating what I said about the experience of playing music with friends being a valuable one whether you make it into a profession or not. I mean, if you go out on a weekend and have fun playing duffer tennis, it doesn't mean that you are heartbroken when Wimbledon goes by without your being on the Centre Court.

A.H.   But do you think it is one of the ways of keeping the symphony orchestra concert alive?

A.P.   Oh yes. Let us even take someone who does not play an instrument, never has done, never will. I think that listening is a talent which can be developed just like playing an instrument can, and I think that this is an area that can either be self-taught or supervised, just as you do often in your work. Someone who is made aware of what listening is about can simply listen better— strange as that may sound—and wind up listening terribly well and finally get a prize for listening,

	a medal or something, and be immeasurably enriched by it, Do you agree with that?
A.H.	Yes I do, but you've got to find the right person to do the teaching. Again, this all ties up with what I was saying earlier about the way music exams are conducted. I once went to perhaps the smartest girls' school in England; I gave a lecture to the whole school in the evening, and the next morning, I had a class of about nine girls who were taking "O" level and "A" level music. I said, "Now here I am, and you can pick my brains; what do you want to know about these set works?" One girl said, "If you can make me like this work it will be a miracle." "What's the work?" I asked, and she replied, "Mozart's Piano Concerto in A, K 488." I was absolutely appalled. I said, "You mean you don't like it?" She answered, "I loved it three months ago, but now we've measured every phrase-length of it, analysed every harmony, we've numbered every bar, and I can't stand it any more." Now that isn't teaching people to listen to music.
A.P.	No, because you are again presupposing that it would do some good to show them the length of the phrase and the bar and all that, and that again presupposes a certain knowledge of music, doesn't it? Were they going to be professionals?
A.H.	No, they were just girls at school, but they were being prepared for an examination. If they had not been being prepared for an examination, there would have been no necessity to learn all these things, except insofar as I believe there are certain aspects of the construction of music which are integral to its drama. If form is taught as the means of conveying drama, as opposed to being a skeleton, then form becomes meaningful. To me the whole concept of Sonata Form is not a

	question of identifying phrases from a piece of music and sticking labels on them, saying this is a First Subject of a Second Subject, but seeing the way in which the composer uses form as a means of creating surprise, or of creating a dramatic situation, or creating a change of mood, whatever it may be. Form in a composer's hands is the same as the masterly use of the stage in a playwright's hands.
A.P.	Yes of course. I think one of the worst things I have found, which I was put through when I went to normal school, is that the music educators in the States at that time were absolutely bloody determined to put a programmatic meaning onto every piece.
A.H.	Now that's a new one to me.
A.P.	Oh yes, even for the Beethoven Fifth we had our heads crammed full of what it all depicted, so that it took years to throw all that out of my head.
A.H.	Tortelier tends to do that, you know. When he is playing unaccompanied Bach, he's got little stories that go with all the passages. "Here," he says, "Bach goes into the next room and says goodnight to the baby."
A.P.	Nevertheless, I think he suggests it rather than teaches it as a fact and that's the difference. I think that it's one thing to tell the story of Till Eulenspiegel and what the E flat clarinet depicts at the end, because that really was Strauss's intent; but to take a normal symphony, like the G minor Mozart, and make up a kind of *Coronation Street* to it, is just unforgivable.
A.H.	But Cortot's interpretation of some of the Chopin preludes is a fantastic instance of this. Have you come across them? He has analysed all the Chopin preludes in terms of happenings.
A.P.	Young listeners—this is really what we are

38

talking about in terms of the future of the concert world; never mind the talented performers or the budding geniuses or even the budding rank and file players in an orchestra, I am talking about the people who will eventually have to replace the old people in the concert hall. I can't tell you how heartening it is to me that in England at this particular moment anyway, during my concerts with the LSO, I have been told that the new influx of young people—and by that I don't mean children but people let's say in their twenties—is noticeable. Well that's fine, nothing could make me happier, not any string of good notices could make me happier. I hope they can be given to understand that the existing snobbisms about which they read are not valid. I talked to a bunch of young people at the Guildhall School of Music and said to one of them just at random, "Be absolutely honest, what's your favourite piece of music? When you go home and you want to put on a record, what do you put on?"; and the young woman blushed, giggled, twisted her foot around, whispered and I had to put her through all kinds of things before she finally blurted out, "Oh God, I'm afraid it's *Scheherazade*." Well, good Christ, *Scheherazade* is a masterpiece and the fact that people write it off on their learned typewriters is no criterion at all; and if someone had said to me "Strauss waltzes", well damn right, you know, that's marvellous. I find it difficult to believe when a fifteen-year-old says to me, "my favourite piece in the world is *The Art of Fugue*." I don't believe that and he mustn't pretend.

A.H. One last point about young people. Here we are in Bucharest, having these fascinating conversations, and around us, not very far away down

39

the road, the Georges Enesco competition is going on. As soloist last night, you had Radu Lupu, who was a winner of the Leeds international piano-playing competition; as a result of that win, his entire career has probably moved forward substantially faster. At the highest level, what do you think is the value and the function of competitions? Do you think they are misleading, or do you think that they are an essential stepping-stone in a very commercial world?

A.P.   I think they are all those things. I have judged on very few out of choice, I don't like to. There are certain competitions whose history is almost flawless, the Leventritt is the best one I know. But—I wish that the competitions would make the following concessions to reality. One is that it is not necessary every single year to give a first prize. If there is a year where contestants appear who play very well indeed but don't bowl you over, then give second and third prizes, special prizes, tie them for second, tie them for third, but I think the first prize in any competition must be given to someone who is head and shoulders above the rest.

A.H.   What you really mean is "who is ready to accept the responsibilities that the winning of the first prize brings", because it usually means playing fifteen concerts in different countries.

A.P.   Exactly what I mean and I didn't have the wit to think of it. That is right. There is a competition in the United States which is well thought of and a few years ago they gave first prize to someone who I thought was just a very adequate pianist. During the course of the first season of engagements which were his prize, he folded . . . and I have never heard of him again. It was cruel to give him the prize. The winner must have not only fingers ready for fifteen concerts, but his mind and his body and his attitude must be prepared for that kind of life, which is not the glamorous life that everyone makes it out to be in romanticized novels, it's a damned hard life. It means travelling and being away from people you love and leading a rather monastic life—studying too much and keeping odd hours and eating awful food and never getting your laundry back. Of course the music is always a great reward, but the periphery is very trying. Once in a while it is great fun. For instance, last night when we met musicians who also happened to be here—and we went out and sat around till three in the morning and told a great many stories and went through the street laughing loudly; that's a great bonus. But I freely admit that that happens one night out of fifty, and the other forty-nine are lonely and boring. Very few eighteen-year-olds are ready for that. Still, that is part and parcel of being a professional musician who tours, and every professional musician does tour. Now Radu Lupu was ready for it, the people from the Leventritt have all been ready for it; but I think competitions are too ubiquitous these days. I think every group of well-meaning people who get together and organize a "festival" or competition are kidding themselves, and what is worse, misleading young people. There are only, I would guess, a dozen competitions that really and truly mean anything, and the rest are manufactured, sometimes for un-admirable reasons.

A.H.   Yes. Do you think that one of the problems which we've got to face up to is that the spectrum of available music is becoming very much larger? It's partly due to the gramophone, partly due to musicologists, and of course the fact that we happen to live in the twentieth century as opposed to the nineteenth or the eighteenth or the seventeenth. You see, I feel that one is in a sense almost overwhelmed by the amount of music there is. Now these festivals try to make a very searching test of a player's all-round ability by stipulating that he should play music from such-and-such a period by such-and-such a composer and of such-and-such a technical standard; there is a tendency for the demands to be so searching that they eliminate completely the type of pianist who, let us say, is a marvellous Beethoven player or marvellous Chopin player, but who is not going to play Bartók well. Now, there *is* a place for these people in musical life. Let's face it, there are pianists that you and I could think of who one would go to hear play Beethoven, but would never wish to hear play something by another composer from another period.

A.P.   Actors who join a rep company might be very good in Shakespeare but pretty lousy in a Feydeau farce: nevertheless they learn and perform both parts, and I think that if someone is at the formative stage in music, I don't mind the requirements being that stringent and that varied, because I think eventually he will find the area in which he is most competent. I don't think that to play the piano, to play the violin, to write music should be a competitive business. I think the only person you should compete with is yourself over the years, and I cannot say that piece X is a better composition than piece Y because they are in two different styles. If I hear someone play the Chopin F Minor brilliantly, I cannot say that he is less good than the person who just played Beethoven Four brilliantly.

A.H.   That was a wonderful story you told me last night

	about Rosina Lhevinne going to a recital by Van Cliburn . . . you remember?
A.P.	Yes; Rosina Lhevinne went to a Van Cliburn recital and afterwards people rushed over and asked what she thought of him and she said, "He's a wonderful pianist but he's no Van Cliburn," one of the most wicked remarks I have ever heard.
A.H.	I don't think it's wicked because I think it's a very good commentary upon the grotesquely angled publicity which comes out of these competitions giving us all a distorted sense of proportion. As John Lill, who won the Moscow Piano Competition, was saying to me the other day, with a touch of bitterness in his voice, "I'm just the same pianist that I was two months ago."
A.P.	But you can get even more specific than that. Suppose Van Cliburn, who by the way is a very good pianist indeed, had won with the very same abilities and with the same repertoire, not in Moscow but in Kansas City, he would still be struggling for community concerts in North Dakota. He happened to win a prize in Moscow at a time when it was absolutely the ideal moment in history to win a competition in Moscow. Let me finish this subject with the following story. One of the rare times when I was adjudicating a competition in the United States, we, the judges, heard a great many pianists. They were competing for a prize which consisted not only of appearances with various orchestras but also the chance to study with a great pianist (whom we shall let remain anonymous) during the summer months at a summer music camp. There was one girl who played the required material very badly but I thought I detected the makings of a very interesting musician in her, so I asked her what she most liked to play. She said, candidly, "In point of

43

fact I don't like what I've had to play for all of you today; I wish I could play Debussy's *Pour le Piano*. We let her play it to us and it was most beautiful. Well, we couldn't give her one of the official prizes, but at least we saw to it that she attended the summer music school and studied in master class with the great pianist I mentioned. Not only was the girl touchingly grateful, but her parents came around, profuse in their thanks, and complimenting all of us for seeing through the nonsensical elements in the competition, and so on and so on. They all went off in a miasma of happiness. A few months later, the same parents came looking for us with fire in their eyes. They had decided to surprise their little sixteen-year-old with a little visit to the music school, to see how she was getting on. Upon arrival there, they were told that their darling was just then with *le Maître* at his home, taking a lesson. And they went there and she was indeed taking a lesson because she was in bed with him. Come to think of it, perhaps she was giving a lesson. Teaching can have interesting fringe benefits.

A.H.   Did you know Leschetizky married five of his pupils . . . ?

A.P.   Good for him . . .

A.H.   We come now to the period of our respective twenties, although needless to say they don't run on exactly parallel lines. In 1939, I arrived at the Royal College with a sheaf of compositions under my arm. I had written quite a lot of music considering I had had virtually no tutoring at the time. A Fantaisie for piano and orchestra, a Concertino for piano and orchestra, several violin sonatas, songs and so on. Inevitably, my college life was a curious one, because it took place during the war. It was an extraordinary time to be living in London, and I wouldn't have missed it for anything. But of course it did mean that one took one's studies very casually because there was no real sense of competition. One didn't believe honestly there was any future. Still, I did manage to win the top prize for piano playing, which was really a bit of a farce, so I'll tell you about it. It taught me a lesson about programme-building, because I chose a programme which was so easy that my friends just rolled about laughing when I told them. By some incredible luck Irene Scharrer was the judge. She was a pianist of great musicianship who was looking for the very qualities which I could give. The day the awards were announced, I went and looked at the bottom of the list, and then I turned away from the noticeboard thinking, "Oh well, I didn't get anything." About ten minutes later people were coming round and congratulating me on winning the gold medal. I said, "Don't be ridiculous, I can't have won it." But it showed that you've got to choose pieces that suit you. Well then, after that things happened very fast and in the most unexpected directions, because I came very much under the influence of Michael Tippett at Morley College. He taught me more about music just talking over café tables than anyone had ever done up to that time. It so happened that he was asked to write the music for Marlowe's *Doctor Faustus* for a production in Liverpool, a commission he accepted only on condition that he got someone else to do the orchestration, because he was too busy. He asked me whether I would do this orchestration. So I waited for weeks and nothing happened. I kept on asking him, "Can I have a bit of music to get started on." Still nothing happened; finally he

	said to me, "I don't want to do this, you do it."
	And so there I was, faced with the prospect of
	writing quite a substantial score for *Faustus* . . .
A.P.	For what kind of orchestra?
A.H.	Just nine players. But there were something like

A.H.   Just nine players. But there were something like
fifty-four music cues. The first night was a sort
of nightmare, because the group was conducted
by a little man who used to play Palm-Court
music in the Adelphi Hotel in Liverpool. He
conducted with a knitting-needle. The trumpet
player had a blister on his lip, so he decided he
couldn't play any high notes; all my most
brilliant fanfares were transposed down an
octave, and not too accurately at that. About
halfway through the play, the players had got so
confused by the beating with the knitting-needle
that they were beginning to play different
numbers simultaneously.

A.P.   Why a knitting-needle—out of eccentricity?

A.H.   I don't think you could buy a baton in those days.
I don't think he had one and so he used a knitting-
needle. Anyway, this led to a lot more com-
missions, believe it or not, and I found myself
earning a living by writing incidental music for
radio and the theatre. The curious thing is that I
was not prepared for this in any way. It had
nothing to do with what training I had had at the
Royal College of Music. It had nothing to do
with anything that I had planned for my life.
Now you've done something of the same sort,
because you didn't really plan to end up being
conductor of the London Symphony Orchestra
did you?

A.P.   Well, in a curious way, yes, I did. I had always
planned to be a conductor but the problem was
that through procrastination and cupidity I let
other things get in the way. As I told you, I did

enter for some scholarships and prizes and competitions and I invariably came in second which is, in it's own way, much more disheartening than coming in last . . . because you can focus your jealousy on one person rather than the whole system. To the best of my knowledge, the first-prize winners have never been heard of since but some other people who were in those competitions who had not even been placed in the top five have become quite successful.

A.H.   These were competitions in what field, in piano-playing, conducting or what?

A.P.   In piano-playing and composition. Anyway, when I was twenty, I wasted two years in the army. It was peacetime and I felt ludicrous. I think that if by some magic fountain of youth I was once again eligible to be drafted into the American Army to go to Vietnam now, I would really simply say no and take the consequences. But in those days I went and merely wasted my time. By now, I only remember the more farcical aspects of it and not the dread of it. I had already done some films and a funny incident occurred. We were out on manœuvres and I was in point of fact digging a latrine trench when an orderly came running out and told me that I had been nominated for an Academy Award. There was something really absolutely hilarious about this because I simply could not care at that point, so I said to him, "Go away and let me get on with the important business at hand."

A.H.   This was a nomination for doing what?

A.P.   For writing the music to a film called *Three Little Words* which has thankfully been forgotten.

A.H.   It has not been forgotten. I saw it and I remember it to this day. I adored it. It starred Vera-Ellen, whom I worshipped.

A.P.	That's right, the thinnest girl in the world.
A.H.	Well if that's thin, that's how I like it . . .
A.P.	Well, anyway, that was the first big film I had done. I had been a nameless orchestrator for other people up to then. Those were days when there were still quite a few Hollywood composers whose claim to composition rested solely on their ability to whistle little tunes to more sophisticated souls who could then write them down, develop them and orchestrate them. I worked for one man—a kind, nice man—whose lack of musical knowledge was awe-inspiring. I think he could have found middle C on the piano only if it had been magnetized and he had been wearing rings. By the way, he was the only man I ever met who played the piano not with one finger but with just one thumb. It was creepy to watch. I remember on one occasion his banging away at the top octave of the piano and saying to me that he wanted the trumpets to play the tune. I said, "Surely not in that register, an octave and a half above high C?" And he said, "Oh yes, yes, trumpets," and when I said as gently as I could that I didn't think they'd get up there, he said, "Well, try, kid!" and ran out of the office. So I had been orchestrating and arranging and ghost-writing when a very kind gentleman named Robert Sisk asked me to compose the score for a film he was producing. He was a distinguished man who had been connected with the Theatre Guild in New York, and he had bought a screenplay by Marjorie Kinnan Rawlings, who had been a Pulitzer Prize winner. Well, she must have written that screenplay to pay off a bet, because it was simply indescribable. In a parlour game today you couldn't come up with the cast of that film; not even as a joke. The three stars were

Lassie, Jeanette MacDonald (in her last appearance) and Lloyd Nolan. It was a terrific break for me, because there was almost no dialogue in the picture. A lot of barking, an occasional song, endless scenery, and the background music never stopped. After that I wrote about ten more movies of the same deathless calibre, then *Three Little Words* and I was drafted.

A.H. I told you that *Three Little Words* made a deep impression on me. I am probably right in saying that you saw Olivier playing Oedipus in New York; well, I did the music for that. To work with a company where Michel St. Denis did the production, John Piper did the décor, Olivier, Ralph Richardson and Sybil Thorndike played the three leading parts when it's your second-ever job in the theatre is to start at a pretty good level. And the same year I had my first one-act opera done at Sadlers Wells so this was a real vintage time for me; I was in my middle twenties, since when I have gone into a state of decline.

A.P. Well I don't think so. No; those are much more laudable efforts than mine were. I did do concerts, I did study, I did work quite hard but I must admit that too much of my time was spent on film music. And I did—you know there's enough anecdotes there for six books.

A.H. Shall we have just enough for a quarter of a book?

A.P. Well, the second movie I ever did was a picture called *Scene of the Crime* which was a film with Van Johnson as a very tough New York cop. It was a police melodrama and the man who was producing it was a kind of distant relative of Louis B. Mayer's. He called me up to his office and he said, "I want to use as a theme a Mexican folksong called *Cielito Linda*." Well, I was

49

nineteen and I was shy and I went away, and back in my own office I thought why the hell did he want *Cielito Linda*? I looked at the picture again, then I went upstairs again and I said, "Listen, I don't doubt that there may be some great allegorical implication that is escaping me, but why in God's name a Mexican folksong?" And he beamed at me and said, "Because it's my favourite song."

A.H.   A very good reason.

A.P.   Yes. Things like that you could never fight. There was another film in which the hero and heroine had to be at a chamber-music concert and the producer said to me, "I want there to be a piano involved"—and he said, "Now, a quintet; just remind me, a quintet is a harp and what else?" And I explained that him, to so then he said, "Well, get something very good." I asked the principals from the MGM orchestra to record the first movement of the Schumann quintet with me. We spent all day at it. It was rather fun, and as was the custom, you then had to send a record up to the producer, and the producer called me the next morning, very excited. He said, "Listen, that piece is absolutely terrific. I'm crazy about it, it's so pretty." He said, "It's so pretty in point of fact that I think we're wasting our time doing it this way and I want you to do it with a full orchestra." Well, I said, "Wait a minute, that's not possible, you wanted it as a quintet." He said, "You can start out that way, then just sneak in a great big orchestra." I tried to explain the meaning of the word "quintet". I talked about Schumann and so forth. He finally interrupted me; he said, "Look here, it sounds like a bunch of shit with five guys, now do it the right way," and he hung up. So I then had to go upstairs and fight a small battle and I was in point of fact taken off the movie because I said, "I won't do it."

A.H.   I'm glad to hear it, it's sticking to integrity. I had a rather amusing episode when I was making *Decameron Nights* with Joan Fontaine and Louis Jourdain. The producer wanted a very loud noise at the beginning, so I had not only the standard orchestra but about twelve extra brass and about five extra drums; naturally I thought it would be rather nice to use them somewhere else in the score so I booked all these players for one session in the morning. The first thing we did was record the title music; the producer was very happy about it, and I thought, "Well this is fine." So I said, "Now we'll turn to 6M1,"* which was a battle-scene. There was a lot of rustling and the players said, "We haven't got any music." I said, "But you must have," because I could remember scoring it. But no, nobody had it; they had copies of every other number in the picture, but they didn't have a copy of that. I suddenly had a horrible sinking feeling in the pit of my stomach, and I reckoned that 6M1 had never reached the copyist. Very quietly, out of the corner of my mouth, I said to the orchestral manager, "Will you ring up my wife and tell her to look in the bathroom cupboard" (which is where I kept my manuscript paper for some strange reason) "and see if she can find anything labelled 6M1." He came back a few minutes later, and said, "It's there," so I said, "Well get it to the copyist, but quick!" They sent it to a copyist in Charing Cross Road, where six people worked on it, and the parts for full orchestra arrived after the lunch break. I never said a word to the producer; I just kept the players back and recorded the whole fight sequence that afternoon. But it was one of

* Reel 6, Music Cue 1.

those nasty moments when you just couldn't say, "I'm terribly sorry, I left the music behind in my bathroom cupboard."

A.P. Yes, well, there are endless things like that. Curiously enough most of the amusing stories I think are based on someone's illiteracy . . . which is a shame but even in its own way, there was a kind of a style, kind of a dash to the illiteracy in those days. It was the last gasp of the old Hollywood.

A.H. The golden era . . .

A.P. There was a composer named Herbert Stothart and he had written some very successful operettas in the 'twenties and had become a motion-picture composer and he was absolutely phenomenal. He had a leonine head of white hair, he was extremely distinguished looking, he was a great *bon vivant*, everybody loved him—but he had absolutely no idea about the technique of music. Everybody worked for him. What he could do was to write very attractive little melodies for movies, old-fashioned but very nice. On one of his latest films he hired me to orchestrate and to ghost-write. He gave me this little rather innocuous melody and he said, "I tell you what I love and what I would like you to copy for the title music—the ending of Respighi's *Pines of Rome.*" So I went home and it was great fun. I absolutely piled it with clashing, crashing sounds one on top of each other with organ just for the bottom notes. When it came to the recording, the score of course was of no use to him because he could only read treble clef; and so they used to make little melody sheets with the timing cues which he was brilliant at catching. Well, the piece started, incredibly grandiose and loud and awful and the producer was in the seventh heaven,

and of course I was tactfully on the bottom step of
the rostrum with the score in case somebody made
a mistake so I could call it up to Mr. Stothart who
would then pass it on to the player. About two-
thirds of the way through, he was conducting like
a windmill, with great happiness ; then he leaned
down to me and in a great stage whisper he said,
"Did I write this?" Anyway I went through the
Hollywood thing in my twenties and had great
fun and made friends. Some of the musicians in
those orchestras were wonderful ; a lot of them
played in the NBC orchestra with Toscanini. Many
of the brass players had played with the great
dance bands. I learnt a great deal and I met a
great many talented people. At that time I was of
the age where being in that ambience is such fun
. . . and you think it's going to go on forever. I
think it was Gertrude Stein who once said, "It
was an age when everybody was twenty-four."

A.H.   Yes . . . there's something there which intrigues
me, because you said you were sitting on the step,
following the score. Now, after one horrible
experience with the very first score I ever did for
radio, I decided then and there that I would never
let anybody else conduct an incidental score of
mine again because it would save so much time if
I did it myself. And I found that this was a
wonderful, practical school in conducting. To
have to synchronize with a picture, so that you
got the thump on the bass drum at the exact
moment when the body dropped after 2 minutes
$31\frac{2}{3}$ seconds was a marvellous technical training.
It meant that the conducting part had to be quite
automatic, because one was thinking about a lot of
other things like synchronization with the action.
Now surely you conducted all your own scores?

A.P.   Well of course I did, I conducted everything that

I ever wrote when my name was on the screen; but don't forget that we are still talking about an earlier date in my life, when I was about eighteen. I was a nameless, faceless person who used to write for this "great man", and what's marvellous is that people used to come up and congratulate him and he used to say thank you and beam with genuine pride, having forgotten that he hadn't written it. The orchestra boys knew it—which is why the next year when I got up in front of them it was not with total fear and trepidation because at least they knew that whatever it was, good or bad, I had written it. I went through a curious series of stages: I wrote for a thriller, and so after that I did about ten because everyone said well if it involves being scared get Previn, and then I did a musical, and then I did endless musicals after that. And then I did a comedy for Billy Wilder and suddenly I couldn't do anything but comedies, and there is a tendency in Hollywood to type-cast like that. It's like poor Miklos Rozsa, a fine, serious composer. He did biblical pictures, and he kept doing them and those are always four-hour epics with an interval, and two and a half hours of music. I remember once that he was near tears at lunchtime, and I asked what the matter was and he said, "Well I've just been given *Ben Hur*. It's the eleventh biblical picture I've done in a row and I simply don't know what to write any more for that man carrying that thing up the hill!"

A.H.   That's the nightmare side of it as opposed to the enjoyable side.

A.P.   There is a great deal of enjoyment. I have now not done a movie in a great many years and I don't miss it very much. Scores now being assembled by pop groups simply don't interest me.

A.H.　　But it's almost as if the wheel has come full circle because it has gone back again to pop groups, who are, a lot of them, musically rather illiterate.

A.P.　　Yes ... but there is one great difference and that is that the illiterate people in those days, the early days, used to try and hide it and cloak it. Now they come out and say, "By God, I don't read music and I don't write music and I don't want to be tied down to the content of the film," and there is a kind of defiant pride in the fact that they can't read, and I have always wondered why that is suddenly so attractive. Anyway, I left MGM and became a freelance composer and did very well. I won the Academy Award four times and I was nominated fourteen times, so you could also say that I lost ten times.

A.H.　　Was the serious music progressing at all at this time?

A.P.　　Yes I was playing a lot. I was playing endless chamber music. I was playing concertos with orchestras like the Boston Symphony or the New York Philharmonic.

A.H.　　What sort of repertoire?

A.P.　　Well I played Prokofiev's Third and Rachmaninoff-Paganini, the Beethoven Three and the *Emperor* and lots of Mozart.

A.H.　　You weren't making it easier for yourself anyway.

A.P.　　No, I wasn't making it easy and I enjoyed all that. I was also taking conducting lessons with Monteux, and I studied with Castelnuovo-Tedesco. I worked very hard but I cannot help but admit that I did it around my other schedule, and it wasn't until I was thirty that I was able to look myself in the mirror and face it and say you are wasting your time, you must admit it. And I then cut down on film work and gradually cut down further and further.

A.H.   To take you up on something you just said, I have found it virtually impossible to make the grade at all in this country as a conductor, although in fact I think from the work that I have done with amateurs and from some very nice reactions from professional players, I have got something to offer. But in England, unless you are prepared to banish yourself to the BBC Northern Orchestra for five years, you cannot be accepted as a conductor. We tend to be put in boxes, and I've been put in the "talking-about-music" box now for quite a long time. Now, some people say that one of the reasons for this is that I never actually bothered to go and study conducting properly. You said you had conducting lessons with Monteux, who is one of the great men of the century. Now to what extent do you really believe that conducting can be taught? I remember both Ormandy and Haitink have told me that there is no way of learning conducting except by conducting.

A.P.   That's true. What I learned was things like reading a score at the piano. What I learned was ferreting out that which seemed important in a complex score. What I learned was simply the atmosphere of an orchestra, and what orchestra players were about, and being around Monteux, and studying whatever he was conducting that week, to be ready to act like an assistant—which I wasn't.

A.H.   You see, I was at the concert the other night, when you were doing *Firebird*. I enjoyed the performance enormously. But I am always wanting to learn from people, even the simplest little technical things. You know at the end of *Firebird*, where that glorious tune comes in the brass, and you have to beat 7 or 11 or something? I've often looked at textbooks which give a little diagram showing how to conduct 11, so I watched you to check how you did it. Well, you conducted it exactly the way I would, which is to make a lot of small precise gestures in the air and try to get the next down-beat clear. But did you in fact ever feel the necessity for acquiring what I might term an orthodox technique ... of a textbook kind?

A.P.   There were certain things that Monteux showed us. Not the very complicated metres but simply like a slow 6/8. He said, "I prefer it this way because its clearer to the men," and so on and so forth. But we were free to disregard it. He never really said, "This is the way you hold the stick," and that kind of silly basic principle.

A.H.   When you said something about the reaction of the men to the beat, I've found that the people who have taught me so much, both when I was writing music or when I've been conducting it, have been the orchestras who play it. Every time I wrote a score for the radio I used to go round to the players and say, "Is this playable, is there any way this passage can be improved, can you do it?" Those were the people who taught me. As for conducting, I would have no compunction in actually asking the leader at any time, "Is what I am doing quite clear?"

A.P.   Oh yes, Tony, I've done it all my life. I did it yesterday morning and I hope I always will. Yesterday, one of the second violins came to me and said, "There is a moment in the Schubert where you do a rather complex small rallentando and you have a tendency then to give the entrance to the cellos, and we cannot see your down-beat so could you kind of flick at us at that moment." And I felt that that was not only sensible but very good of him to tell me, and so I made a little mental

57

note and when the time came, I gave a little flick with my left hand and they all came in quite correctly. Now I would not have known that as a practical necessity if the man hadn't been nice enough to tell me.

A.H.   May I tell you something which exemplifies my attitude to conducting? I was asked to spend a day at the Guildhall School of Music, taking a conducting class. During the morning, I was discussing a flute entry in Tchaikovsky Fifth, and I said to the group, "What is different about this entry of the flute from any other entry in the movement?" They all tried to think of way-out things like "It should be louder", "There should be room for a crescendo", and so forth. Not one of them had even a clue as to what I was searching for, and they were obviously quite bogged down. So I told them that the difference between this flute entry and the ones all round was that it was the only one that came after forty-six bars rest. You see they were only looking at the one page, and not thinking about it from the flute-player's point of view. Would you agree that the conductor has got to learn to identify himself with the players, and to ask himself, "What do they want from me?"

A.P.   Oh yes. Monteux used to say, "Before you impress the ladies in the audience make sure the horns come in right." The LSO and I used to go to the Florida Festival in the summer, which we did four years running. There was a student orchestra and there were master classes run by Ashkenazy and Perlman, and I used to conduct the student orchestra a lot and there were a couple of people who wanted to be conductors. There was one boy who was very gifted, I felt, and he mentioned to me once quite *en passant* that he thought of the orchestra as a great impersonal instrument on which he would play. And I said forgive me for sounding like the old sage but I think you would be making a rather dangerous mistake to feel that way, because an orchestra is not made of brass, or catgut, or wood or ivory, but is composed of a hundred people all of whom have private lives, stomach aches and bad train-rides in, and whatever else, and that makes up how they feel that day.

A.H.   And who also think they know the music better than you.

A.P.   Who not only know the music better but more than likely have played it more often than you've conducted it. And I told him he must not think of it as an impersonal thing. And he said, "Well nevertheless, I think it is better for a conductor to think of it totally impersonally." At that point Barry Tuckwell had come to pick me up to go to the beach. He called me over and he said, "Why don't you let that young man conduct us for about ten minutes one day," and I asked what on earth for. He said, "Is he talented?" and I said, "Very", and he said, "Well, we haven't eaten a young conductor alive in months!" So I put the boy up on the LSO rostrum and of course he came off shattered, because the LSO simply had destroyed him. And I think that the lesson was harsh but not invalid because I think he found out that you are not dealing with an inanimate object but you are speaking to a hundred very good musicians, and that it is very difficult to cope with all the personalities in front of you.

A.H.   One of the things that I used to say to young composers at the Royal College was that if you are going to write a piece of music which makes extraordinary demands on the performing capabilities of performers, either by its rhythmic complexity or by the newness of the sounds which you expect it to produce, you have got to be an even better all-round musician than the people who are to play it. You have got to know exactly how you want it to be done. It's no good just sticking something down on paper and hoping it's going to work. You have got to be so sure because you are really making a terrible imposition on these people. I remember once being told by Neville Marriner that he was in a string trio that was asked by the BBC to play a short work by a modern young English composer. This was a work which took about six minutes to play, and these three top-class professional string players rehearsed it for about twenty-six hours, at the end of which they still didn't feel safe. So they said to the BBC, "Can we record it in sections of 15–30 seconds at a time."? Now it is my view that a young composer who writes a piece that makes that sort of demand for such a very dubious return is arrogant.

A.P.   I find that disgraceful. You see, something that I admire beyond words is, for instance, the fact that Benjamin Britten, who does not play the cello, writes like the most extraordinary cello virtuoso; he does not play the guitar, but writes brilliant guitar pieces. Of course all of us have a working knowledge of the more common instruments, but you know, Bream and John Williams were telling me that Britten really can't play anything, and yet the parts go to the limits of virtuosity, but they are never impossible, and that is admirable . . . beyond compare I think. To continue what you were speaking about—that conductors in England have to go through a rather stiff apprenticeship before their name is known at all. When I decided, as I mentioned, that it was time to call a halt to the incessant film activity I had a very peculiar problem and that was that in certain music circles I was rather well known, except I was well known for the things I wasn't ambitious in. Hollywood used to abound in what we call rehearsal orchestras. Those were orchestras made up of studio players who had all been in the major symphonies and who simply couldn't stand playing junk day after day; they used to get together once a week in some school auditorium and just read through things. Every once in a while they did a concert; well, I conducted one in which I did standard repertoire and there were two people in the audience by accident who I want to mention by name. One was Schuyler Chapin. He was at one point the head of classical recordings for Columbia. He was then the Programme Director for Lincoln Center and he is now managing Leonard Bernstein's affairs. He is also one of my oldest friends and the godfather of Matthew and Sascha. With him at the concert was a man I didn't know at the time: Ronald Wilford, who is the Vice-President of Columbia Artists, the management corporation. Well they saw me conduct and they took me out for coffee afterwards and they said, "Look here, you should do this. You should conduct. You are a good pianist but there are too many good pianists and you should conduct. The only thing is that you can't conduct as a hobby." And I said, "Well I never intended to." And they said, "Are you willing to cut down very heavily on your motion-picture work, if not give it up altogether? Take an immense loss in money, start travelling like mad and go through all the rest of it?" And I said, "Yes of course I am." Now I am only sorry that it was so late because nowadays the twenty-year-old

61

conductor thrives, it seems to me, and there I was thirty.

A.H.   It was not such a heroic sacrifice as it might be in a novel because presumably you'd got a fair amount stashed away by now.

A.P.   No, it was not a heroic sacrifice at all because no sacrifice is heroic when the gains are bigger than the loss ; I never cared all that much about money. I made a deal with Ronald Wilford. I mention this because although this was ten years ago, he is still my manager, he always will be, I am great friends with him and he advises me at all times, and Schuyler Chapin does too. So I made a deal with Ronald Wilford. I said, "Look here, I may go out and be absolutely dreadful at this, so what I will do is keep to one film this year and let you run me around, and then we'll see. At the end of that year you tell me whether it's worth giving it all up, moving out of Hollywood and really going at it tooth and nail, or whether I should just simply philosophically say, well I'm not as good as I hoped I could be, and then I will go back to the not entirely unpleasant business of scoring films." So he said, "Fair enough." And I then had offers —this is what I was getting to—instantly from Philadelphia, New York, Cleveland, Chicago, Boston. Everywhere : but the offers were to do Rodgers and Hammerstein nights, Gershwin nights, Cole Porter nights, Lerner and Loewe nights. Well, that is in essence what I was already doing except I didn't have to pack and go in aeroplanes to do it. I was very comfortable in the sunshine of California. So I am very happy about the fact that I was absolutely adamant at that time about never succumbing to that particular seduction. I never said, as many of my colleagues in Hollywood with conducting ambitions had

	done, Boston Symphony, oh boy I can't wait, you know,—Koussevitzky, all that history—and then they got up and conducted . . .
A.H.	*Rhapsody in Blue* . . .
A.P.	Right—or Gems from Rodgers and Hammerstein.
A.H.	You interest me when you say that; I'm surprised that an orchestra like the Philadelphia Symphony would play that, because I doubt if the LSO would.
A.P.	No; but the American orchestras all have a pop season during the summer. All the outdoor places, for instance the Hollywood Bowl, the Robin Hood Dell, the Blossom Festival, Meadow Brook, every place. What they do is they have two or three serious nights a week, and then one or two pop nights with the full orchestra; which is where people like Henry Mancini and John Green and Meredith Wilson give their concerts. Well anyway, I never succumbed to it and I said no and I told Ronald, "What I want to do is Brahms, Britten, Bartók and so on." And he said, "Fine. I will map out a possible tour for you, the biggest city of which will be Kalamazoo," and away I went. Here was the point. These cities had semi-amateur orchestras or semi-professional, depending on whether you are a pessimist or an optimist; they were glad to have me come and conduct because people saw my name and were hoping I would either play the piano or do something from the movies. So they would come and hear me. Once they were locked inside the auditorium and I started with Haydn, all they could do was groan with hatred. But they had already paid you see, so these orchestras wanted to hire me, especially since I was asking a fee that barely covered the plane trip. And I did that for quite a while.
A.H.	But it is in fact the only way to learn the repertoire.

A.P.   Yes, I knew the repertoire better than some, but
not from a practical point of view. And I did
work—I have to say—terribly hard those years,
not just in terms of uncomfortable travelling but
of incessant studying, I mean hour after hour,
night after night. And there, the fact that I had
stood in front of orchestras, professional orchestras of great standing, and conducted them for
many years, helped me a great deal. The fact
that the music had been film music had given me
a very fast rehearsal technique and it had given me
a knowledge of what orchestral players can stand
and what they like and what they don't like. So
off I went and after that there was no great
glamorous story. I worked hard, the orchestras
got better, the engagements got bigger and then
finally I was able to do the big orchestras. But it
did take me, not only the years of provinces but
also years of overcoming a specific kind of
geographical prejudice against me, because the
word "Hollywood" in the United States is
beneath contempt when used in any connection
with serious music, unlike in England where
everybody does films and is happy to do them.
For years when I went to a city and conducted, if
the next morning I looked at the review and the
first sentence started out by saying, "Last night
Hollywood's André Previn etc," I never finished
reading it, I give you my word. I would put it
away because I could already reel off what the
rest of the damning evidence would be. And the
way I overcame that was simply by going back
again and again, and no journalist can afford to
hang his hat on the same tired peg year after
year. So finally I remember very well that first
time I got a bad review simply because the critic
hadn't liked the concert, not because I had been

in Hollywood. I remember being terribly pleased and thinking that I had finally made it. By now, of course, the films are so old and the jazz records so forgotten that I think I am being judged only on how good or bad last night was.

A.H.　To me, one of the greatest excitements of this whole world of incidental music, in which we both have done a fair amount, is not only the immediacy of the experience, but also the whole technique of recording film. It is so different from the world of concerts. There is all the dubbing, the balancing and the synchronization, and I find the idea of conducting a symphony orchestra with a cinema screen behind it appeals to two elements in my character. I am sure part of me would have liked to have been an actor. I love words, which I suppose leads me to do so much writing and speaking; there is also another part of me that wants to be a composer and conductor and a musician and so on, and they both seem to meet in the recording studio when one comes to the point of making a film. I think what I miss most of all about not writing film music nowadays is the actual recording on the day.

A.P.　Yes, I have great fun recording, and I always look forward to it. There is that moment in the middle of the second or third day of a big score when the next cue comes up and you are working fast, and my librarian hands me the next score and it is in my handwriting, and I have absolutely no recollection of having written it. I don't know the tempo or what it is for or what it is about or anything, and that is an absurd moment.

A.H.　I had a strange experience not long ago when a film for which I had written music at least fifteen years ago came up one Sunday afternoon on television. It was intriguing because I could not remember one single note; I couldn't even remember where the music was going to begin or end. I listened to it as though it had been written by André Previn in fact. But it was an extraordinary experience to hear this "child" which had been nurtured at some time or another come back into one's life as a completely anonymous stranger.

A.P.   Many of the films I wrote very early in my career have now come back to haunt me on the *Late Late Show* on American television. Sometimes I'll look at one of them for a few minutes and a great many memories come rushing at me; not memories of the music itself, but of the circumstances under which the score was written. Places and events and faces, rather than notes. I must tell you that I usually wind up cowering behind the furniture with embarrassment at my own ineptitude when I hear old efforts of mine. What amazes me is that I must have thought the music good at the time I wrote it; what's more, the people who paid me must have thought it was at least good enough. Were we all mad, or deaf? Have standards changed that much in film music, or in myself? Of the fifty-odd scores I composed for Hollywood, I can listen to, at most, ten without cringing.

A.H.   Well that is perhaps because you were so young when you did them.

A.P.   No, because the studio which hired and paid me was certainly not in the habit of encouraging young talent. They were not given to saying, "That's very good, considering the composer is only eighteen." They wanted their money's worth.

A.H.   But weren't you selling them what they wanted? Didn't they want awful music?

A.P.   Perhaps, in certain circumstances.

A.H.   Do you reckon in theory that the relationship between the composer and the producer is something which can be artistically productive, or do you think that it is always going to be a fight between conflicting interests?

A.P.   Since I have started doing so-called big movies, I have worked with a great many famous directors. I have never once had a fight with a director, and if I disagreed with him to any degree I have never once encountered a director who was not willing to discuss it and come to terms. However, I have never thought this kindly of producers. Now I think a producer is a little different in England. Am I correct?

A.H.   Let us get our definitions right. The producer is what one might call the office man. And the director is the chap who says, "Cut" and lines up the shots.

A.P.   Yes. The director is the man who actually makes the film. The producer is the one who handles the money, the distribution and all that.

A.H.   Yes.

A.P.   It has only been producers whose musical outlook has ever rattled me enough to walk out on several big projects. The last time was only a few years ago. I was enamoured of the idea of making *Goodbye Mr Chips* into a musical film, but everything fell to pieces when I started to talk certain points of aesthetic to the producer, a man named Arthur Jacobs. It was, of course, my own fault. I should have known when I saw him move his lips as he read the script, that he wasn't the right collaborator. It was hopeless and I walked out. On the other hand, I did five scores for Billy Wilder, who directs, writes and produces himself. I never once had a musical discussion with him that did not show his sensitivity and dramatic shrewdness in the use of dramatic music. I've learned from every good director I ever worked with. There are, unfortunately, brilliant new film directors who simply don't believe in music. Mike Nichols is a good example. I think he feels that music in a film can only be justified if it has a visual source, such as someone turning on a radio or sitting at a keyboard. Years ago, Hitchcock told Alfred Newman that in his film *Lifeboat* he wanted not a note of music. "After all," he said, "where would the orchestra be coming from, in the middle of the ocean?" Newman had a nice answer. "From the same place you got the cameras." Anyway, I like working with directors a lot, but producers, no. Producers and tenors are, generally speaking, to be avoided.

One more opinion, if I may. Some of my colleagues in Hollywood make it a practice to concoct suites for concert use out of their movie score material. I don't think it ever works. Please don't remind me of Prokofiev's *Nevsky* or Walton's *Henry V* because those are the exceptions proving the rule. Most film music, no matter how brilliantly effective it is in conjunction with the visual image, is too devoid of form to stand up in the concert hall.

A.H.   There is something here which I think I would like to get down in permanent form because regard it as being one of the things of which the British film industry really can be proud. There was a long period when Muir Mathieson was the musical director at Denham, where most of the movies were made at the time. One day he said to me, quite seriously, "I regard it as my privilege in this job to be able to use films to subsidize all the worthwhile British composers by giving them

68

the chance of writing films." Now this meant that in this country, we had film scores by people ranging from Benjamin Britten, Arthur Bliss, Lennox Berkeley, William Walton, Richard Rodney Bennett (of the younger generation), John Ireland, Vaughan Williams.

A.P.   John Ireland?

A.H.   Yes. John Ireland wrote the music for a film called *The Overlanders*, a film about Australia. It was a very good score. All these people wrote film music which added very considerable lustre to the film industry. It meant that the quality of film music in this country was probably the highest in the world. In the States, it seems that very few of the really accepted composers, apart from Aaron Copland, ever produced scores for films, or is that a wild statement on my part? I can remember Virgil Thompson's *Louisiana Story* which was a documentary, but it was a marvellous score.

A.P.   Aaron Copland won his Academy Award for the score to *The Heiress*, and a wonderful score it was, too. However, William Wyler, who produced and directed, thought Aaron's title music too harsh and dissonant and wanted it re-written based on a tune called *Souvenir d'amour*. Copland refused, of course, and his music was thrown out. Two arrangers were called in, they wrote a nice orchestration of the desired tune, and when you next see the film on television, take notice of a musically really wild first five minutes; after a few declamatory seconds of Copland's comes a very soupily sentimental arrangement of an awful melody; then quite suddenly, after perhaps three minutes, Copland's unmistakably personal music shines through again. In those days, composers had rather unprotected contracts, and any mayhem could be committed on their music.

A.H.   Let's leave films for the time being. What made you decide to come over to England, because this must have been a pretty big step to take?

A.P.   It started in 1965. RCA sent me over to conduct some recording sessions with the RPO: concerto accompaniments. I loved working in London, and requested that I record here again. Roger Hall, who was then in charge of classical recordings at RCA, was most sympathetic, and I was sent over soon after to record the Tchaikovsky Second and the Shostakovich Fifth, this time with the LSO. They liked me well enough to offer me several concerts, both in London and out of town, and so I began conducting them quite often, in public and on more records. I must tell you a story, which sounds so patently like the concoction of a publicity agent that you must promise to believe me when I tell you that it is totally true. Do you know a radio programme called *Desert Island Discs*, which the BBC has had on since, approximately, the year 1795?

A.H.   Indeed yes.

A.P.   Well, I went as a guest, and the final question Roy Plomley put to me was: "All conductors have some ultimate goal. Which of the world's orchestras is your goal? Boston, Philadelphia, Vienna, which?" And I answered, "To tell you the truth, the best orchestra for me, on every level, musical and otherwise, would be the LSO. I know it's presumptuous of me, but some day, before I'm in my seventies, I'd like to have that orchestra." When I said this, I genuinely had never considered it as anything but an eventual dream. Six months later, the LSO invited me to become Principal Conductor. That day was the biggest day of my musical life ! I was, at the time, music director of the Houston Symphony, in Texas. I had succeeded Sir John Barbirolli there. It was a fine orchestra and I was happy conducting it, but the offer from the LSO was truly the end of the rainbow for me and I simply leaped at it. Of course I called the management of the Houston first, and promised them that this new post would not interfere with any of the concerts in Texas. I kept that promise, too, for more than a year, although it meant commuting from London to Houston practically on the same scale as I commute to my home in Surrey now. I was a beloved figure at Heathrow, believe me ! I still think the airlines owe me some kind of medal.

A.H.   Did nothing ever go wrong ? I think one of the great fascinations about air travel is that the margin of error is so wide. You only have to have a small cyclone or something, and you find yourself being landed 800 miles away from your actual destination. Did you never find yourself conducting in Geneva instead of London ?

A.P.   No, but I had my luggage go to Rio with scores in it while I was en route to Chicago. I was really travelling excessively during those years. I was conducting all over the world and never really unpacked anywhere. Then I noticed that every time I landed at Heathrow, as soon as I stepped foot on the ground, I was happier and more relaxed, calmer and more settled. A drive through the countryside seemed to cure all my ills. I couldn't wait to move permanently to England, buy a home, and settle down. Even though I might have been able to keep up my Texas–London run for a few years more, I came to the conclusion that I would only be happy here. So I made that rather big move. I cannot imagine living anywhere else, ever again. You grew up here; perhaps the things that strike me so forcefully don't hit you in quite the same way; but to me, waking up in the Surrey countryside, with silence, green silence, all round me, is a thrill that renews itself every morning. Of course, professionally speaking, London is the most important musical centre in the world today. What Paris was in the 1920s to literature and painting, London is to music now. I can reduce that to a personal feeling again: in America, I always felt that the artist is considered a kind of luxury item, available only to a privileged few. Here, in England, I feel that all of us, performers, composers, interpretive or creative artists, are a daily necessary part of everyone's life.

A.H.   That was a pretty substantial change of direction in your life. I went through a rather similar metamorphosis when I was about thirty I suppose, because I virtually stopped writing incidental music for the radio, once television began to take over in a big way. Suddenly, I found myself being employed more and more to talk about music. The only way I can remember all this starting was that I had done a few isolated programmes when a producer called Roger Fiske, who knew a great deal more about music than I did, said to me one day, "If you had *carte blanche*" (and this is just like your London Symphony Orchestra story) "if you had *carte blanche* in broadcasting, what would you choose to do?" I answered, speaking straight off the cuff, "I'd like to have a half-hour programme every Sunday evening, in which I could talk about one work which was being broadcast that week." He said, "Would you really?" and I said,

"Yes." And I heard nothing more about it for about six weeks. Then there arrived a contract to do precisely that. At first, it was just for three months; then it grew to six months, then nine months, and now this programme has been going for very nearly twenty years—which is a lot of broadcasting. I have discussed over six hundred major works in this series, which maybe isn't as much fun as conducting them. Still, it is preparing the ground for people to come and listen to a conductor performing them. I am wondering whether a good deal of the credit for this musical climate that you find so attractive here, is not due to the consistently educational policy at the BBC. From what I can gather, in American radio the bulk of the material that goes out is not really presented in what one might term an illuminating fashion; someone just says, "Here is the something-or-other Golden Hour of Music" and out comes a record of Toscanini conducting the NBC or whatever it may be. Well, the BBC perhaps more than any other radio station in the world, has made a positive effort to go on educating people, and although perhaps I have had a good deal more than my fair share of this particular job, there have been plenty of other people who have done a lot too.

A.P.   It is very possible that the kind of insistence on good music in the mass media in England is responsible for the incredible concert audiences here; incredible in size and in enthusiasm.

A.H.   Yes. Can we talk a little bit about this? A lot of people say that music is an experience which is not convertible into words: if this is true, I shall have to throw myself out of the window, because I have been wasting my time. I believe that the average person, who goes to concerts or buys a

73

gramophone record for pleasure to listen to at home, feels that there is some key to the mystery of music. They reckon they are getting part of the message, but they can see from the involvement of the artist who is performing that there is an intensity which burns within such people that is denied to the ordinary listener. They think that if there is someone who could open that door, they might feel the warmth of that flame that much more intensely.

A.P.　But what could be better as an ambition?

A.H.　I agree it is a good ambition: but I feel the average approach to the appreciation of music barks up completely the wrong tree. If you read the average programme note for example . . .

A.P.　I am not musically intelligent enough to understand programme notes and I am the first person to admit it. I don't know what the hell they are talking about more than half the time. I will prove to you what I am saying is true. Mel Powell, the composer, and I, were talking about just this, and he suddenly laughed and got up and fetched a programme and said, "I am going to read to you the programme notes of a work that you know very well and I want you to tell me what the work is."

A.H.　That's a good party game.

A.P.　And he read me the programme notes. I said, "Read that last bit again" as I couldn't even follow it, so he read me the last part again, all about the reversal of the stretto coda half-based on the germinal motto . . . and I said, "I haven't the faintest idea." Mel screamed with laughter and said, "It's your own piece." It was my *Symphony for Strings*. I hadn't the faintest idea what that man was talking about. Also, when I then examined it closely, he was simply misin-

74

formed. I mean he misinterpreted, because the things he gave me credit for were certainly laudable but they hadn't entered my head.

A.H. Well, you see, I feel that the person who buys a gramophone record and reads the sleeve, or the person who goes off to a concert and reads the programme notes, has been led up the garden path by these mystical prophets of jargon. What is your feeling about the idea of popularizing music in the base sense of the term? How does one find the middle road between saying, "Beethoven was a great composer, and listen to this", or writing the really totally obscure type of programme note?

A.P. I don't think it is as necessary for the music itself to be more popular as it is for the act of listening to music to be more popular. Once the desire to hear music is instilled, the individual response to further information will vary greatly. I'm not sure that I would be enthusiastic about the idea of detailed historical and musicological facts becoming all that "popular". I feel that way about painting too, for example. On a Sunday afternoon in any of the great museums, the Metropolitan or the Tate, when you can see hordes of bored, recalcitrant children standing around, or running through the corridors, or trying to touch the canvases with sticky fingers, while the unfortunate guide drones on and on to them, then I get very worried about the so-called popularization of fine art. I don't particularly want people to feel that art can be assimilated so simply. On the other hand, I would love for them to understand that music is not made on holy ground, that one does not have to come immaculately tailored to a concert, or drive up in a Rolls ; I would like them to know that music is a

75

commodity as easily available as the cinema, but not as easily understandable.

A.H. I tend to think that it is *too* easily available. I have this idea that you can just turn a switch at home, and out comes the most profound work that Mozart ever wrote; in the middle of it, the telephone rings and so you switch it off. I regard this as artistic vandalism. I remember hearing a broadcast by a man who must have been in his seventies, who, when he was young, had walked thirty miles to the Three Choirs Festival to hear the first performance of Elgar's *Dream of Gerontius*. He described how the mere fact of having to walk thirty miles gave something special to that performance. It was like a pilgrimage, a spiritual purification before what he knew was going to be the summit of artistic experience for his entire life up to that point of time. One of the great dangers of the mechanization of music nowadays is that we can come to regard it as being a convenience, like electric light or central heating.

A.P. I hope you won't think me cynical, but the man who walked thirty miles to the concert was prejudiced in its favour long before he got there. Quite naturally too. After such an effort as his, he would not allow his mind to think of it as anything but a sublime evening. Therefore, he got a lot out of it. I know that if I have a very hassled time getting to a concert, if I have had to rush from work, and have had to fight the traffic and probably have forgotten my tickets, and have been shown to the wrong seat, and so on and so on, then I finally want my reward for all that trouble. Psychologically, you can will a better performance than you might actually be hearing. There's nothing wrong with that.

76

A.H.   But surely this contradicts what you were saying earlier about wanting music to be easily available, and people not having to dress up?

A.P.   No, I meant that segment of people who wouldn't dream of coming to a concert whether it was easily available or not. There are people now, especially young people, who still think of the concert hall as the last bastion of nineteenth-century establishment, and of old dowagers with canes sitting in the box sneering . . .

A.H.   Not at the Proms, they don't. They queue for five hours or more.

A.P.   Yes, but the Proms are unique.

A.H.   As an American coming to England, presumably, with pre-conceptions about English musical life, was your first Prom really a revelation?

A.P.   Well it was what the kids now call "an enormous ego-trip", because I remember that at the end of the performance—I think I had done Walton's Symphony No 1—there was the kind of outburst which one would hear at a football game. I was so unprepared for it that it really frightened me. The enthusiasm, afterwards, of all the kids was incredible. It has happened to me every time since then; and if I watch the Last Night of the Proms now on television, I get truly tearful about it and so does my wife. We sit there and weep at the enthusiasm of the kids with the very 1970 placards, and the fact that they are swaying and singing *Rule Britannia* and meaning every word of it. It's beautiful. But the Proms have to stay out of a discussion on musical supply and demand because I don't know anything like them in the world.

A.H.   But the Proms to us are something which are very English, and yet to anyone outside they are something which is terribly un-English.

A.P.	Well I don't think so. I think it is very English.
A.H.	We have touched a little on the question of your change over from what one might term the more commercial side of music to the world of orchestral concerts. To what extent do you think that Leonard Bernstein has been responsible for musicians coming to accept that it is possible for someone to contribute to both worlds?
A.P.	I think he was instrumental by simply being such a strong personality that he overcame the stigma that was attached to Broadway and to his interest in popular music. I think he changed the attitude towards popular musical theatre considerably. He has of course written a great many successful Broadway shows.
A.H.	Yet perhaps the best score he did was the unsuccessful one, *Candide*.
A.P.	Yes that's true. But it's successful in terms of music. I have only written one show for Broadway, and planning on another one next year; and it was Lennie who made it possible for a serious musician to write in the more popular genre. I am reminded of a story that Roger Voisin, the principal trumpet of the Boston Symphony told. He said, "My father was a brilliant trumpet player. But he did not understand jazz and he hated it and of course he couldn't play it." He said, "I myself don't understand it, but I like it, but I still can't play it. However, my son is a very good trumpet player and he understands it and he likes it and he plays it." I rather like that. And Lennie has made it possible for individuals such as myself to straddle the fence occasionally.
A.H.	I watched a television programme the other night from Ronnie Scott's Jazz Club in London. And they had a pianist there who was playing what was described as "avant-garde jazz". It was pseudo-

Stockhausen, and frankly I was appalled. I thought that at least one thing that jazz was going to continue to have was some instant appeal. What do you feel about this whole question of the influence of avant-garde music on jazz?

A.P. I must give you a rather evasive answer. To be an expert in jazz, you must have it as an everyday enthusiasm. My own interest in the past decade has been very sporadic and I simply don't know where it's at in jazz at the moment. In the 1950s I was considered a very modern player, and I remember thinking how odd the generation preceding me was with its love of Dixieland. I thought it was so old-hat! Well, here I am now, past my youth, and I find myself still identifying almost exclusively with the jazz of my active years in that field. I am still thrilled and excited by the likes of Miles Davis, Oscar Peterson, Bill Evans, and Dizzy Gillespie, but for all I know that makes me hopelessly démodé.

A.H. But don't you think that it is a little self-conscious, the way in which the leaders of (for want of a better term) "avant-garde jazz" have really gone out of their way to drag in the names of Boulez and Stockhausen and such people on the sleeve notes of the records? They do seem to be making an effort to stand right alongside the big figures of contemporary music.

A.P. Perhaps the musicians are tired of their music being called jazz, since that word usually denotes the opposite of "serious" music. Perhaps their ambitions are higher now; I see nothing wrong with that.

A.H. In a way I find the idea of listening to jazz that seriously is almost grotesque. I went to the famous First Late Prom in which they had a pop group, The Soft Machine, playing; what

79

struck me as such a paradox was to see all those people sitting perfectly still, listening to music which was surely designed to set off a physical reaction. One girl was sitting very high up near the organ-loft, and she was really "sent" by the music; her head and her hair were swinging about, and she was much more exciting to watch than what was going on on stage. I felt that we should have been dancing in the aisles!

A.P.   Well I must say as a man who has played a lot of jazz I would hate it if the audience started dancing in the aisles, but I know what you mean. I think that there has always been a tendency in the so-called serious jazz fan to take his listening to it too seriously. I mean it is more serious to them than the Bruckner Mass; it never is to the musicians. I thought curiously enough that The Soft Machine music was just terribly old fashioned. It was kind of moderately well played, half-way boring 1955 jazz; I saw nothing that would have interested me even then.

A.H.   No. I once made a definition which may seem rather frivolous, but I reckon there are three sorts of music. Music which is aimed at the head, music which is aimed at the heart and the stomach, and music which is aimed at the feet. The greatest music is that which appeals to all three elements. In a classical symphony, the first movement is primarily aimed at the intellect, i.e. the head, the slow movement is primarily an emotional piece, i.e. aimed at the heart and the stomach, the scherzo is primarily a dance movement, i.e. for the feet, and maybe the last movement is a sort of summing-up or whatever it may be. Perhaps this is a slick and glib definition, but to me jazz has always meant music which has a physical appeal, aimed at the feet rather than the head. Now I know that there are plenty of jazz composers who do write allegedly cerebral music, but they don't do it too well.

A.P.   I disagree with you. I think that a great deal of good jazz is aimed directly at the heart. I have been deeply moved by certain improvised solos. I mean emotionally rather than rhythmically.

A.H.   Yes. But the beat is there underlying it all the time, don't you think, even in the Blues?

A.P.   Well, the Blues takes in a lot of territory. I'm not sure that a steady beat is so necessary at all times, in order for it to be deemed jazz. I don't know to what degree of musical sophistication the players have arrived. I remember it was an absolute revelation when people played an occasional piece in five. I don't know whether that is taken for granted now or not. I have heard groups that do collective improvisation, but not collective improvisation à la New Orleans, but collective abstractions, if you like, and I find them mostly self indulgent and boring to listen to.

A.H.   But New Orleans is regarded as a sort of classical period, and therefore it has got a timelessness about it which has given it a continuity. The things that are happening now are essentially evanescent, because the whole atmosphere nowadays is that things become obsolete almost as quickly as they are achieved.

A.P.   Well of course all improvised solos should, shouldn't they, in their own way. You see, having come from what was, God help us, called the bebop era, I still very firmly believe that jazz should swing. That of course means also at the very slowest possible tempo . . . and whether it is light or driving or whatever. That concept, I think, has gone by the board. I suppose I am old-fashioned in many musical matters. I still like

81

music notated in the way that has served composers since the first musical thought was conceived. I find that I am more and more tolerant of music I might have found old-fashioned ten years ago. On the other hand, I will not conduct a piece simply because it is a new piece, that's not enough of a reason. We are all so damned afraid of being termed philistine. That certainly applies to the jazz world. There were a great many people who did not recognize Charlie Parker's genius when he first appeared on the scene. All they heard was that he had a rather offensive tone by their standards. Well, a few years later, after Charlie Parker was officially found to be great, they all had to back-pedal wildly. Ever since, jazz critics have found it safer to adore almost everything that is radically new, whether it is intelligible or not. Some of that is true in our field now because I think as soon as a piece is totally unintelligible, not only to the musicians but certainly to the audience, it is always terrific for some sage to say, "Well nobody got it, but I did." I have always felt that unless I, personally, with my own shortcomings, my own failings, my own lack of education, my own prejudices, unless I see something in the work, I should not touch it. And that is not totally out of self preservation but even if you like, out of some kind of deference to the composer, because there will certainly be another conductor who will consider such a piece another step towards the key to the absolute, and he will therefore bring that attitude to the music and do it much better than I, who would only use whatever available technique I have in getting the right sounds and the right noises and the right notes, but I wouldn't believe it. I don't like to do music I don't believe in.

A.H.   Well I feel the same. I won't do a broadcast about
        a work I can't feel any affection for. I think it is
        an abuse of privilege on my part to unload my own
        prejudices on to a public. Going back for a
        moment to jazz, there is one piece I remember
        particularly that interested me very much—I
        wonder if you've come across it? It's on an LP
        called *Inside Sauter-Finegan* which has got some
        absolutely fabulous arrangements on it; one
        piece is called *Wild Wings in the Wood*. It's
        tremendously influenced by Stravinsky, which is
        the sort of marriage that I find is very fascinating.
        After all, jazz started as the music of illiterates,
        entirely improvised by people who had no
        formal musical education. They played because
        it was a natural expression of their souls, and this
        is how the great world of jazz began back in New
        Orleans. Now when you listen to people like
        Sauter and Finegan, who obviously are immensely
        sophisticated musicians, one finds a sort of
        "bastard" music, trying to have a foot in both
        fields. I am fascinated by it, because it makes
        Stravinsky a more easily available currency;
        but I am wondering whether the end-product is a
        valid work of art. Is it either good jazz, or bad
        Stravinsky or which?

A.P.   I find that I have the most curious and surprising
        reaction to that question, Tony. As I have told
        you, I am not active in jazz, haven't been for
        years, haven't kept up or listened to the new
        boys ... and yet I find that I reacted just now
        completely like a jazz musician. Sauter-Finegan
        never had *anything* to do with jazz and never
        pretended to. Eddie Sauter and Bill Finegan are
        both extremely educated musicians, as you say
        they know both sides of the fence, and they
        decided to put together a band which would be a

showcase for their arranging ingenuity, as opposed to most bands which show off individual players. Within the limitations of the instrumentation at hand, they did some phenomenal things; I don't know the specific piece you mentioned, but I remember very well buying a record of theirs and being staggered by their invention. However, it only interested me for a few minutes at a time, because I thought it was the opposite of what jazz is about and yet not complex enough to be considered as serious music. Even Stravinsky had a brief affair with a big band; he heard and fell in love with the Woody Herman band, as well he might have, and paid them the ultimate compliment of writing a piece especially for them. It was called *Ebony Concerto* and there was a good deal of fuss made about it. As a serious piece it was third-rate Stravinsky, and as jazz it was simply non-existent. He had written a work for the instruments contained within Woody's band, but he failed to understand the kind of noise they could make best.

A.H.   But this leads me to a fascinating link that I have often used in musical appreciation. Suppose I was trying to interest a group of young people in the music of two hundred and fifty years ago. One of the things that I would show them is that just as a jazz player today does not play exactly what he sees before him, so would a seventeenth- or early eighteenth-century musician have distorted rhythms, and improvised decorations—in fact there is much common ground between a jazz player and the seventeenth century. This seems to be a bridge which is worth exploiting if one is trying to get through to the young.

A.P.   Well the sad thing of course is that at the moment jazz isn't in such favour even with the young.

Just yesterday, when we landed at the airport a young man came up, I would say mid-twenties, shook my hand and said, "I am Zoltan"—(I did not get the last name) "I am the president of the Jazz Clubs of Romania", and proceeded to overwhelm me with his knowledge of jazz old and new. Now there is evidently still a lot of interest here, but in America that audience which we who were concerned with jazz in the fifties found the most receptive was the college-age group, and they have now replaced jazz almost totally by folk-singing and pop groups. Jazz has once again retreated to the underground, which it has not done in a very long time.

A.H.   Do you reckon that pop music has the same qualities as jazz?

A.P.   No, I don't. For one thing, it just simply isn't played as well. I can't really discuss Pop and Rock, first of all because I don't know much about it, and secondly because I am appalled by the amount of misplaced intellectualism that seems to accompany all articles on Pop these days. In *Esquire* magazine in America, for instance, or in the local columns of Tony Palmer, there are sentences of such hilarious seriousness about Pop! They discern cosmic philosophies and musical profundities in almost every three-minute collection of twangs put out on records. I enjoy certain Pop music quite a lot, certainly the Beatles are brilliant song writers; but I simply don't see Pop being anywhere near as important in the musical scheme of things as the best of improvised jazz was and will be.

A.H.   When you say it is not important in the scheme of things, it has one importance and that is that perhaps it is the nearest thing to universal music that we have known. I mean, you travel all over the world, and I do a fair amount myself. The fact is that if I go to Bangkok or Hong Kong or somewhere like that, there in the windows are records of the Beatles, and the Rolling Stones or whoever is the latest rave. This *is* a lingua franca; surely this is something fairly significant in twentieth-century civilization?

A.P.   Well, distances have shrunk incredibly; everything is now immediately available the whole world over through the mass media. What is popular in Cleveland, Ohio, on a Monday can be heard in Bangkok the following Thursday. It used to take years for a trend to reach the four corners of the earth; now it takes a few days.

A.H.   Can we leave jazz now, and go on to another subject which I think is very much of our time, and that is the question of music and recordings? You see, I personally rather deprecate the perfection of the gramophone. I have a nostalgic feeling for the old days when playing the gramophone was quite hard work, when every four and a half minutes you had to wind the thing up, turn the record over and change the needle, and so on; at least you were participating in the performance in some way, and more than that, at least you were getting something which was substantially less satisfactory than a live performance. Now, I tend to feel that there is an increasing danger that we will arrive at a state when it's technically possible to have your entire living-room wall filled with a three-dimensional picture, in colour, with very good sound-reproduction of André Previn, aged sixty-five, conducting the London Symphony Orchestra. In the circumstances why bother to go to concerts? I can see a situation developing when there is no longer going to be an audience to go to concerts,

	which in turn will mean that orchestras won't be able to get enough experience to become good enough to make the next film that will replace the one that you have got now.
A.P.	Good God, yes . . .
A.H.	Do you see what I mean . . . ?
A.P.	Yes I do.
A.H.	It's a sort of vicious circle of built-in obsolescence which is going to get worse and worse and worse, because once people stop going to concerts, who is going to make the records?
A.P.	I'm very much the devil's advocate about records because in the first place, it is not possible to be an artist nowadays and not make records. I mean we all owe a lot of our careers to records, and if, when we travel, people know who we are, it certainly is because of records. I also like recording, and I enjoy being in the studios. But at the same time, there is one other thing that I want to add to your recollection of the old 78 r.p.m. days, and that is that because of the fact that the breaks in the movements of various pieces often came at the most inopportune moments, I, for one, used to memorize exactly where they came, and starting, let's say forty-five seconds earlier, I would stand over the machine, absolutely ready, and then whip the record around or off, put the next one on, put the needle down so as to mini-mize the break between. That meant that the attention span was total. Now, with LPs and tapes, you can load the changer with hours of uninterrupted music. It's lovely, certainly, but it leads sometimes into the most extraordinary mixtures of music : I've been at someone's house where the record player is going at a continuous, polite murmur, and have heard, let's say, the first two movements of a symphony, followed by the

last movement of a piano sonata, followed by bird calls, followed by Mantovani, because that is simply how the stack of records has been dropping on to the turntable. The LP has been the greatest advance in recording, and its inherent qualities are endless, but it has also made it possible for music to be playing and *not* be listened to.

A.H.   Well I can give you the most macabre instance from my own experience. I was in Australia some years ago, and I spent an evening in a man's house ; the first reaction that he showed when I came into the room, after offering me a drink (which I didn't accept), was to put on a record. He reckoned that we couldn't possibly talk without having some sort of musical background. The record he put on was Schnabel, playing the Schubert Impromptu Op. 90 No. 1. "This is my favourite record," he said. "Whenever I come home from work I always put this on, it relaxes me, it's such a beautiful piece." And I said, "Yes it is a beautiful piece, isn't it," though I didn't like to add, I wish you wouldn't put it on if we are going to talk. Some months later, he came to my home in London ; after dinner, I thought as a gesture on my part, I would play the same Schubert Impromptu. Afterwards, he said, "That's lovely, what is it?" and he didn't actually recognize this piece which allegedly was his favourite record.

A.P.   Well, that is a hair-raising story but, since I don't know who that man is and since I hope you won't tell me, I like to chalk it up to the fact that the man had what we call a Tin Ear. I don't think that can be ascribed to the fact that one was a record and one was a live performance.

A.H.   No, I wouldn't say it was that ; but I think it suggests that whenever he put it on at home, he was always talking or drinking, or mixing drinks with the ice clinking, or answering the telephone.

A.P.   The perfect corollary to that story is a Schnabel remark. Schnabel was one of the last pianists to record. All his colleagues had already been recording but he had refused. He said, "I have a terrible fear of making a record of a Beethoven sonata and somewhere, some day, someone is going to listen to it while eating a liverwurst sandwich."

A.H.   But to my mind, this is one of the sicknesses of civilization today; you cannot escape through music any more. I want music to be a rare experience.

A.P.   Music is too ubiquitous right now. It is insane. Now, for instance, on aeroplanes, at least in America, they put tapes on not only just before you take off and on landing, but sometimes when the weather gets a little rough, as a kind of sedative. Not very long ago I was flying from Boston to New York and as on all short trips, it was rougher than a long trip, because they don't gain any great altitude. It got very bumpy and suddenly the music went on and it was, I think, Lawrence Welk's Polka Band. The weather really was awfully rough, and I finally called the stewardess over, and I said, "Look here, I know that the odds against anything happening to this plane are probably a million to one, but nevertheless that one must exist because you have put on soothing music." And she said, "Well yes, but I shouldn't worry about it." And I said, "Even at those odds, the last music I hear before crashing is not going to be by Lawrence Welk. I refuse to die to that. Do one of two things, either put on the Brahms *Requiem* or turn the fucking thing off." She backed away from me because she thought I was quite mad. But they did turn it off. The larger thought, that drivel-music would calm a group of passengers some of whom would be in mortal fear, I find absolutely devastating.

A.H.   My psychological approach would be to put on the *Flying Dutchman*. If one had music which really glorified the concept of the storm and made it an exciting experience, we could all crash to our dooms happily, because the music would be right for the occasion.

A.P.   I think that the best thing that they could put on the loudspeaker to make any sense would be the captain saying, "Ladies and Gentlemen, we are landing in five minutes."

A.H.   But seriously, don't you think there is a tendency with the gramophone for people to become obsessed with either one performance—which is the only one they ever hear, or else to become obsessed with just comparing the superficial aspects of performances?

A.P.   What bothers me is the guaranteed perfection. I don't want to be that relaxed in the knowledge that there aren't going to be any mistakes. I don't quite know why, but I think the fact that if somebody puts on a fiendishly difficult piece of forty-minutes' length and you know that whatever has happened during the performance has already been corrected for you, makes the music seem inhuman.

A.H.   Yes.

A.P.   But still, I think the phonograph record is one of the great blessings and I couldn't get along without it, and I have machines all over the place.

A.H.   You see I don't feel like that, because I never play the gramophone for pleasure.

A.P.   Well I do a lot.

A.H.   For me, it's just a tool of my trade.

What about the psychology of conducting for a recording, as opposed to a performance? Surely there must be a radical difference when you know there is a chance of doing a re-take as opposed to going out there on the platform, knowing that if the clarinet comes in wrong you are going to carry the can.

A.P.   Yes. I am sure there is a psychological difference, but I like to think that it is not a terribly conscious one.

A.H.   Which do you prefer?

A.P.   I don't think I prefer one to the other. Recordings have the danger of permanence, and yet simultaneously the comfort of re-takes. They also have the practical luxury of the fact that you can come dressed absolutely any way at all. I think if one had to make records in white tie and tails it would be really disastrous because the work is too concentrated and too repetitious, and there's something about the formality of clothes at a concert which still works, although I for one, like to think that it isn't going always to be necessary for musicians to be penguins.

A.H.   There couldn't be a less practical costume to conduct in than tails.

A.P.   I like to make records. You see, I have been in recording studios all my life in one guise or another, starting at the age of sixteen, literally many times a week, so that the fear people have who suddenly start making records at a given point in their career, I have done with and dealt with twenty years ago. It is possible to pick very detailed flaws at a recording and make sure that they are absolutely corrected and at one and the same time that is great fun and very rewarding. But if you do it too much you tend to lose the performance. I have a habit which not every record producer is happy with, I like to make very long takes. I like to make takes of entire movements and when I re-do anything I will do whole sections. I will almost never re-do, let's say, ten bars. I once watched with absolute amazement, an American conductor who was recording a symphony and who did all the bits with full orchestra first and once those were in the can, he let the brass go, because he then decided that if he now went over time, it wouldn't cost as much, so he literally did all the climactic parts first.

A.H.   No!

A.P.   Yes, a very famous man—

A.H.   The union had really got hold of him—

A.P.   Well, the records were fine. I heard them at the end of the session, but nevertheless, I do think that one should go for the performance. Of course, it would be ideal if everything could be taken care of, but it rarely is.

A.H.   But don't you find a much greater feedback from an audience, and from the whole situation in a concert hall? You come to a concert hall and see a lot of people there; you get a warm reception, then you turn your back on them. At once you are isolated in a world of your own; but afterwards —the excitement, the applause—surely this is something for which the recording studio has no equivalent.

A.P.   Surely, because it is both a musical experience and a theatrical experience. I think there is a theatrical experience, even in being part of the audience at a concert, not just from the performer's point of view, because you have come to a theatre of sorts, and the performers have come on in costume, if you like. I mean it is abnormal for a hundred people to be in white tie and tails, isn't it? Of all people, Rex Harrison once said something very apropos to what we're talking about. He was recording some of the *My Fair Lady* songs, and doing rather badly. Finally, in exasperation, he said, "Damn it I can't do it this way. I have to be in make-up. I have to be in costume, and I have to be scared."

A.H.   Yes; it's a matter of identifying with the part.

A.P.   When an orchestra and a conductor and a soloist are out on stage, there is something in the air that is not in the record studio, but the idea, of course, is not to relax that much at a recording session. It's just a different kind of tension.

A.H.   Do you think the answer is to record concerts, as Richter does?

A.P.   Yes, I would like that very much. I have never had a concert recorded and released commercially. It certainly seems a very good thing to try.

A.H.   If you have got a cough-proof audience.

A.P.   Yes, there is that too.

A.H.   Is this something that has never really driven you frantic? You are in the most beautiful moment of the slow movement of your favourite symphony and somebody has a sneezing fit.

A.P.   No, the human noises, sneezing, coughing and the like, don't bother me. What bothers me is unexpected noise, a door slamming, an audible train passing by, those kind of sounds.

A.H.   Stories about the hazards of live performance lead me to the "spiritual" requirements, if that's not too pretentious a word, of the concert artist. I believe that anybody who can go out and identify himself completely with Beethoven, whether a conductor, solo pianist, cellist or whoever it may be, has to be a person with a very substantial depth of character because, essentially, he is trying to identify himself with one of the great human beings of all time. In other words

93

you can play superficial music if you are a superficial person. If you are going to play great music greatly you have really got to be a great person. Would you think this was true or is it the wrong assumption?

A.P.   I would love it to be true, but I doubt it because I have known several artists who, when they are playing, seem to become great people and the minute they either close the instrument or put it down, are really not terribly worth talking to.

A.H.   Perhaps this could be explained, almost as a sort of spiritualism. The medium is the artist, so to speak; he is in communication with Beethoven while he is playing, and once that communication stops, then he just becomes himself.

A.P.   I wonder if it is absolutely necessary for an artist to be "great" as a human being. I guess it would help, but I mean, for instance, I doubt whether you would have wanted to go on a walking tour with Gauguin or Wagner.

I like to think that an interpretive artist of even moderately high order, should be concerned not only with music but with the artistic striving of other fields too. I don't know a great many musicians whom I admire who are not also fairly well versed in literature and painting.

A.H.   But when you use a phrase like "artistic striving", it tends to suggest that there is a fundamentally athletic attitude about the performance of music—in other words that it is a physical activity rather than a mental one. You're implying that music can be performed by somebody who really isn't up to the mental standard that the composer demands. I feel very strongly that when I am playing Beethoven, however badly I do it, I am making a quite positive effort, not to better myself exactly, but rather to come to terms with

94

the demands which Beethoven makes on me. It's one of the reasons why I feel so passionately about the whole question of listening to music; you can't just have it on as a background. It's like inviting a great philosopher to tea, and saying: "Now sit in the corner and talk to me." While he is talking, you do *The Times* crossword or something quite different, and you don't really take much notice.

As I see it, when I am playing Beethoven, I am, as it were, in conversation with him; I feel I must stop worrying about whether my fifth finger is trilling adequately with the fourth, or whatever it may be, but rather be absolutely in touch with Beethoven's spirit as I am playing.

Now is this just awful pretentiousness on my part?

A.P.   No, not at all. It's most admirable. I think we all feel that way but I think some of it can be self-delusion. You might be in conversation with Beethoven but nobody else is listening to you talk to him.

A.H.   I challenge you on that because I don't mind whether anybody else thinks I am talking to him or not. When I am giving a performance, I like to think that I become so absorbed in it that I forget about the audience. The best performances are those that I give to myself in my own room, alone.

A.P.   Oh, certainly. When I sing in the shower, I am sure I sound better than Caruso. I am exaggerating to make the point. What I really mean is that it is the performer's duty to communicate the composer's intent, and sometimes, if one is not careful, a very personal involvement can obstruct that duty.

Several years ago I was conducting the Brahms First Symphony. The day of the performance I had had some private news of considerable anguish. As a result, I went out on stage and poured all my feelings into the performance, I became totally immersed in the music, and at the end of it I thought I had given a really superb performance, certainly the best of which I was then capable. I came off into the wings, and there was Ronald Wilford, my manager. He said, "What the hell was that just now? What were you doing? That was the most tasteless wallowing around I have ever heard." I was furious. I could hardly speak to him. Luckily, that performance had been taped, and the next morning I listened to it. It *was* the most tasteless wallowing around I had ever heard.

A.H.   You weren't in touch with Brahms. You had made it into the First Symphony of André Previn.

A.P.   No, I thought I was more in touch with Brahms than I had ever been. The point is that you should not necessarily be in conversation with Brahms when you are performing. I think rather you should be his voice saying his ideas, not your own voice answering him back.

A.H.   I wouldn't quarrel with you for one moment on that. Of course I appreciate the fact that the artist is a medium. He is a communicator; he's just a middle man between the composer and the audience.

A.P.   Well that's why being a composer is such a damnable thing because until that middle man is around, the music doesn't exist.

A.H.   Which is why I think that an artist, a painter, has a very much better time of it than a composer. A composition means nothing until someone brings it to life by a performance. Whereas an artist, however bad the painting may be, has created something which is solid and permanent; there it is, and you can hang it up on the wall, and either throw darts at it or think it is the most beautiful painting in the world.

A.P.   If you buy a painting, let's say by Francis Bacon, you have bought a creation and a performance. Every time you look at it that work is performed for you. Not only do you own the performance, but you even own the work it is performing. If you bought a manuscript of Stravinsky's for the same amount that they charge you for a Francis Bacon, you wouldn't own the work because that is still owned by the publisher and you certainly wouldn't own a performance of it because it is just paper. You would just be buying the world's most expensive autograph.

A.H.   Yet I have talked to artists about this, and they don't seem to have this feeling about their painting. They tend to say : "I've lost interest in it. It's over for me. I want to get on to the next one." And I too, of course, have had this about my own compositions many times. I feel after I have written something, not exactly that I have fallen out of love with it, but I have lost interest in it, and I don't want particularly to care about it.

A.P.   Well I can prove that, at least for myself. When I conduct one of my own works, I have it less committed to memory than the most casual piece of anyone else's, and that is because when I have written a piece, when the last bar is finished, I am so bloody relieved that it's over that I won't really study it as a conductor. I will put it away and suddenly I'll pick it up in order to conduct it, but I won't work through it with a conductor's eye. I never memorize it well at all, whereas other people's music I make a point to remember.

A.H.   Yes. It is a very strange attitude this of the creator towards the thing he has created because it seems to be very different from what one might term a maternal instinct. The instinct of the

	mother to identify herself with children is not shared by artists on the whole.
A.P.	Well, I have to clarify something here : I am not a composer-conductor, I am a conductor-composer. I am just putting it into the right order. I am a conductor who composes. I can't speak for full-time composers because I think the order of importance is reversed for me.
A.H.	But there are many composers who are quite incapable of conducting and give very bad performances of their own work.
A.P.	Yes, but nevertheless, I think that composing is so much more important than conducting. I get very uneasy when I read about any performer, be he ever so brilliant being called a genius, even if we are talking about Rubinstein, Richter, Karajan, anyone. I don't like the word genius misused, because—this is going to be a blanket statement, to be disagreed with if you like—I don't think any interpretive artist is a genius ; just creative artists can be.
A.H.	But this doesn't prevent an interpreter from also being a genius as a creative artist. Take someone like Rachmaninoff. Now he was, surely, a supreme example of somebody who was perhaps the finest pianist of his age and also a magnificent conductor and a great composer. Don't you think that if Rachmaninoff hadn't dissipated his energies in conducting operas for quite a long time, he might have been a better composer?
A.P.	No, not necessarily, but if someone were to ask me why do you consider Rachmaninoff a genius, which indeed I do, it would be for his compositions much more than for anything else.
A.H.	Well now, you must be aware of the weaknesses in Rachmaninoff's compositions which the critics have picked on.

A.P.   Certainly I know the weaknesses in Rach-maninoff's music and I know the weaknesses in Shostakovich's music, but nevertheless these are not expendable people. It is so easy to say : "Well there are certain cheap tendencies," or whatever else is the "in" phrase of the year ; but these are not composers who can simply be put aside. It all seems to go so cyclically. There was a period not long ago when no one would admit that Tchai-kovsky was a great composer but they certainly do now, and Sibelius was in and now he's out and coming back in slowly ; I mean, it's all so trendy and fashionable. When I am conducting a work, even if I don't totally agree with it—let's say I don't even like it very much, if the composer is there then I will be deferential to every single wish he has.

A.H.   I find when I am arguing about things like this that I am so aware of blank spots in my own make-up. For example, I find it very difficult to cope with what I call "long" music ; perhaps I listen too intensely. I have a little gremlin seated in the back of my brain, like a shorthand typist, who will insist on taking down everything that I hear as I am listening. It isn't that I have flawless ear and am able to identify every single harmony or every single sound, but I have a damn good try ; this is one of the reasons why I find that when I am listening to music by Mahler, Bruckner, or Wagner, to name the three most specific in-stances, I get musical indigestion very quickly. I love any consecutive quarters of an hour of Mahler, Bruckner, or Wagner, but I find the whole work very difficult to take. Just as I find it difficult to take three string quartets in a row. If I go to a chamber music concert, I'd rather hear two string quartets and go out, than try and listen to three and come away feeling exhausted.

Now this, you could well say, is something which is a sort of intellectual perversion on my part. Perhaps I should relax and just let the music wash over me, which, perhaps, is how you ought to listen to Bruckner, Mahler and Wagner; but the point that I want to make is that a professional musician must necessarily listen to music in a totally different way from an amateur.

Do you feel that the composer is writing entirely for a hypothetical professional audience in his mind—that he expects them to be aware of everything that happens?

A.P.   I think he is writing for himself.

A.H.   In which case, to come back to Rachmaninoff, I find it almost unbelievable that he could have such technical expertise at his fingertips and not see the flaws.

A.P.   But look, how do you explain Beethoven's *Jena* symphony or *Wellington's Victory*? Everybody is entitled to a few lapses. I don't think that's so important. By the way, I don't agree with you on Mahler or Bruckner, but Wagner, at least at this particular stage of my life, mostly defeats me. I think there is more music in any ten minutes of Berlioz than there is in the entire *Ring* and I'll send you the mail I will get as a result of such a statement.

A.H.   Well I'll send it back to you because I agree with it. To me, Berlioz is one of the great gods of music. One of the reasons for this is that I identify myself so completely with him as a man. After all he wrote the greatest autobiography of all time as far as musicians are concerned. I know the book so well that I feel that I identify myself totally with his struggles and his aspirations; if he writes something that doesn't quite come off, I feel I'm there beside him, sharing the sort of horror in his mind, realizing that it wasn't quite as it should be. I feel Berlioz is such a *human* being, which I certainly don't feel about Wagner.

A.P.   No, certainly not about Wagner, but there are people who genuinely do. It is impossible not to admit, for instance, that the first few measures of *Tristan* changed the face of music for ever and ever. There are moments in Wagner where you just sit with mouth agape, awestruck that anyone had composed such music, but nevertheless, as a whole it's almost impossible for me to identify with the atmosphere which he liked in his work, all those Norse gods, and all that. It's very difficult for me to sympathize.

A.H.   One of my favourite cartoons of all time is of two operatic singers on the stage with the curtain still down, and they are wearing what I call full Wagnerian kit—helmets with horns, and string tied round their legs, and swords and shields and so on ; one of them is saying to the other, "Good Lord, they're playing the overture to *Carmen*." This is perhaps a rather oblique way of getting into the world of opera, but since we have mentioned Wagner, we must. Do you have aspirations to be an operatic conductor?

A.P.   I have aspirations to do opera, yes, certainly, but not to the degree that some of my colleagues do. Some of them, certainly Zubin Mehta, basically like opera better than anything else and I basically don't. I love the symphonic literature and its endless variety too much, and I find it depressing to think of all the music that I will never in the world get to conduct. If I conducted non-stop twenty-four hours a day from now till I drop, I'd never get through a lot of music which fascinates me and I am much more interested in that than I am in opera. Certainly I am looking forward to my work at Covent Garden, but if I thought I was going to spend the major part of my every musical day listening to opera singing, I would not be happy.

A.H.　But with your involvement in films, you must have a lot of feeling for the use of music and drama simultaneously. I have the theatre in my blood to a very strong degree, not through inheritance, but because of the fact that so many of my early experiences were theatrical ones. I wrote music for about twelve or thirteen productions at Stratford. I did music for Olivier's *Oedipus*, and, as I told you, Marlowe's *Faustus*. Marlowe, Shakespeare and Sophocles are pretty good writers to be associated with, apart from the fact that the whole atmosphere of the theatre appeals to me enormously. I can honestly say I have lost count, but I have written around nine or ten one-act operas now of the chamber kind. From the composing point of view, I think the idea of writing opera is one of the most fascinating of all, because you have got to fuse so many different arts into one. I would have thought of all the conductors that I have ever met, you would be the one who would, perhaps, be best equipped by nature and by upbringing to be an ideal operatic conductor.

A.P.　There are any number of operas that I would adore to do. I will always be ready to do them. Any one of Mozart's. I think *Figaro* and *Don Giovanni* are the two most perfect operas in the world. I would like to do *Fidelio*, I'd like to do some Russian opera. What I don't like is the kind of opera that is called "grand opera", a very nineteenth-century velvet curtain business; but I think that when it comes to a leaner kind of musical drama like *Peter Grimes* and *Wozzeck*, that fascinates me. Yes, I am terribly interested in musical drama, but then I think there is such enormous musical drama also in non-singing music.

A.H.   A lot of people think that opera is on the way out. Do you think the symphony orchestra is on the way out? A lot of composers behave as though the symphony orchestra is practically a dinosaur now. When they do use the symphony orchestra, they divide it up into sections and have a series of small groups; you know the type of thing. Do you think that for the talents of someone like you, the theatre does hold a prospect? Suppose you could find a way of working in a completely new art form that was neither opera nor a musical, but was a dramatic experience in the theatre which involved a musical expertise of a greater degree than has been provided by anybody so far, except straight operatic composers?

A.P.   Well, who could turn that down? You're offering a Utopian concept for a composer. Of course there have been many unclassifiable works involving theatre and music already. You can't call *West Side Story* a musical comedy, not if *Oklahoma* is also one. It was a great cut above all that, in musical conception. Menotti's *The Medium*, or *The Saint of Bleeker Street* were not exactly operas, but they weren't musicals either. Honegger's *Joan at the Stake* is another example. There have been quite a few works which defy categorizing, but many of them are damned good.

A.H.   All the same, one shouldn't conclude that the critics are always wrong.

A.P.   Oh, no.

A.H.   They have a contribution to make, but do you think they have a contribution to make as far as the performer is concerned? I feel that to read in a newspaper that a concert took place last night, and such and such a work was performed either well or badly, is an extraordinarily futile waste of time because the performer is not really going to take much notice, or benefit from it. The people who went there certainly aren't going to benefit much, because it is all over now, and the people who didn't go are either going to say, "I wish I'd gone", or "I'm glad I didn't", so what good does it do?

A.P.   I think that it is difficult for a performer to be entirely fair about critics because so often you run into lamentable situations. Now the most recent occurred only the day before yesterday.

We were in Bucharest, and for many reasons we were unable to start the programme as planned with Robert Simpson's Third Symphony and it was announced that we would, instead, start with something else, the Sea Interludes from *Peter Grimes*.

The next day there was a review in detail of how brilliantly the Robert Simpson symphony had been played, and how clear I had made music never before heard. The review went on for quite a while. And also, the next night, the Kirov Ballet danced and there was a great review given to the ballerina, who had, in fact, defected in London the previous week. With these two events so fresh in my mind, I have a tendency just simply to write off criticism. On the other hand, on those occasions when one reads a great home truth about one's own performance, then it is different and very valuable.

A.H.   But surely, in his heart of hearts, an artist feels, when he reads a bad notice, that the man who wrote the notice is wrong?

A.P.   Of course.

A.H.	So, therefore, does it in fact have any constructive use?
A.P.	Yes. Sometimes, when you're having a sleepless night and thinking with cruel clarity, you review things that have been said about you and you find truths in them. However, I must say that if a performer has been at his profession long enough, he is almost always the best judge of his performances. I can generally tell whether I have done a good or a bad job. In a strange way, it is almost as disheartening to get a good review for what you know to have been a bad concert as it is to get a devastating review for what was truly a good one.
	Obviously, I would love it if everyone adored everything I do, but they're not going to, and I really haven't got the time or inclination to worry about it. I have a terribly busy schedule, and the morning after a concert I am already starting to prepare the next one, and the night before is over and gone.
A.H.	I tend to keep the awful ones because they make me laugh more. They can sometimes be very entertaining, so far away from what one imagines one has done—
A.P.	Ned Rorem, the American composer, said to Bernstein, "You know, Lennie, the trouble with people like you and me is that we want everybody in the world to love us", and Lennie said: "I'll tell you why that isn't possible, Ned, because it will never be possible for us to meet everybody in the world."
A.H.	I became disillusioned with criticism actually, not with regard to anything as transient as a performance, but with regard to one of my printed compositions. Now you would think that when a critic has a composition sent to him to cover for one of

the musical monthlies that he would have a fair amount of time to mull it over and give a considered opinion. Well I once had a piano composition of mine reviewed simultaneously in two monthly musical magazines ; I kept and treasured those criticisms for a long time. The first one (which naturally was the one that I agreed with) said that this was a work which was written extraordinarily well for the piano, full of the most ingenious invention in the way it handled the musical material, and that it should be in the repertoire of every self-respecting pianist.

The other one was so much a mirror inversion of this that it was really funny, because almost in exactly the same order of events the critic said this piece was *not* well written for the piano, that it singularly lacked invention of any type and that he couldn't conceive why any pianist should want to play it. Now the point that one really had to decide was which one was right—or were they both wrong?

A.P.   It's hopeless. I mean, we've all got stories like that.

A.H.   But about performances, surely, rather than about something which is so concrete as a piece of printed music.

A.P.   No, I don't think so.

I think one of the most amusing forms of music criticism is in magazines which specialize in recordings. I must say that the American reviewers are much more guilty of it than the English. Many recorded performances are now no longer available, and so there is a tendency for reviewers to play safe by the following method. Let us say that a terribly famous conductor—shall we say Karajan?

A.H.   Yes.

A.P.   All right, let's say Karajan has recorded the

Eroica again. The reviewer spends a little time on it, says what's good and bad, but then comes his ace-in-the-hole: "However, actually the only close to idealized performance of this work, albeit badly recorded, is by Hermann Kupfermeyer on Belgrad Records, mono only, unfortunately not available in this country since 1927." Well, poor old Karajan—once again second-best to something that cannot be checked.

A.H.   Well, it's a good way of covering yourself, isn't it?

A.P.   The best one ever was by someone on the *Saturday Review* in the United States, who compared someone's performance of the Tchaikovsky Fifth to Toscanini's performance, and how Toscanini's was really the only time it had ever been perfectly played. He got a flood of indignant mail saying that Toscanini had, as a matter of fact, never done—the Tchaikovsky Fifth. The reviewer then apologized as follows: "I stand corrected. However, I am familiar with Toscanini's work and had he ever done the Tchaikovsky Fifth, it would have been better than with this performance."

A.H.   I detest being called a critic. If I was so reduced in circumstances that I had to be employed by a newspaper as a critic, I would say: "I will do so only on condition that I may write the notices for the concert before it's given," and my notices for the concert would read this way. "If you are so fortunate as to go to the Festival Hall this evening, you will have the opportunity of hearing a piece of music by such-and-such a composer." I would then write an article about the piece of music, and aim to make people really want to go and listen to it. I might also say, "You will hear such and such a pianist who, in my opinion, is one of the great artists of our time, and this may be the last

	chance you have of hearing him"—or something like that.
A.P.	But you'd still be stuck with a new artist and a new work occasionally.
A.H.	Yes. Well, in which case I could still surely chance my arm and say, "Have a go at this, because it is the sort of experience you ought to submit yourself to."
A.P.	Surely that would be doing away with criticism?
A.H.	Wouldn't I be lifting its function considerably?
A.P.	You would be changing it totally. I think one of the functions of the critic is simply to be a good writer. For instance, when Virgil Thomson was one of the critics in New York, I used to read his reviews with great pleasure and I even bought them when they came out in collected book form, because even at those times when I vehemently disagreed, they were written with charm, wit and a deftness of phrase, and I enjoyed reading them as essays.
A.H.	Bernard Shaw was a great music critic, but he certainly wasn't a great musicologist or musical scholar.
A.P.	No, but one can read those reviews still with pleasure. I like someone to be a good journalist while he is being a good critic.
A.H.	When you were saying that in American schools there was a great stress laid on programme music, or rather, a false interpretation of symphonic music into programmatic terms, it strikes me as strange that you should be so keen on the music of Richard Strauss. Now Strauss is almost entirely programmatic, and yet you appear to deprecate a programmatic approach.
A.P.	What I resent is non-programmatic music being turned into programmatic music by those people who run that abhorrent course known as music

	appreciation in American schools. They decide that in the Beethoven Fifth, it isn't enough to talk about the music, they must tell you, "now at this point visualize the rushing river and the animals running through the forest," and all this kind of crap; that is what bothers me. I resent a programme being straitjacketed on to abstract music.
A.H.	When you say music appreciation is abhorrent to you, you are giving me a tremendous stab in the back! My approach to music appreciation is a different one, because I don't try to read other things into the music; but one has to use analogies or metaphors at times, in order to make clear in words an idea which has been expressed in music.
A.P.	Forgive me. What I meant was, while I was in school in America, the courses known as music appreciation, which were part and parcel of the curriculum, were run in a manner so as to guarantee a life-long hatred of music and I was referring to that specific part of my education.
A.H.	Yes, which obviously failed in your case because you managed to survive it.
A.P.	It failed in my case because I was so insulted by it that I failed the course.
A.H.	Anyway, if I may return to the appreciation of music, my feeling is that its real function is to make the listener share the composer's purpose and to become identified with that purpose in such a way that one feels that one is almost watching the piece unfold as it is being written. What I try to do when I am talking about music is not to impose something from outside, but rather to say to the audience: "Looking at the music, this must be the way the man's mind worked." Now, surely, to do this sort of thing is valid because it is letting them into the mystery of composition, but doing it by a purely musical door rather than by

	an analogist's door. I do feel that there is an awful lot to be said for trying to make people share the creative experience.
A.P.	Yes, so long as it's in hands such as yours, it is a laudable concept. But it can be mishandled so viciously, you know, that I think it is dangerous to put literary values on music.
A.H.	Talking of literary values, it appears that there were certain composers in the nineteenth century whose whole aesthetic approach towards music and its function was changed by literature. Liszt took copies of Goethe and Dante wherever he went; Berlioz was a fanatic for Virgil and for Shakespeare; such men allowed these literary concepts to spill over into their music to such a degree that they really became a substitute for the pure formal characteristics which had been sufficient for composers like Beethoven, Mozart and Haydn. Some nineteenth-century composers obviously felt the need for some sort of programme. They felt they were bringing something vitally new to music by writing, shall we say, a *Faust* Symphony as opposed to a symphony in C sharp minor.
A.P.	I see no harm in that, do you?
A.H.	In a way, it could be said to be a sort of betrayal of the art. It could be said to reveal a certain lack of confidence in the ability of music to speak for itself—a little bit as though an artist were to say: "Well here is a beautiful picture, but I want you to listen to a piece of background music while you are looking at it or you won't get the message."
A.P.	Yes. Cartier-Bresson, the great photographer, put the best of his life's work into one huge expensive volume, and then on the cover is a Matisse, and I always wondered why a photographer would put thirty or forty years of photographs into a

	book and then put a painting on the cover.
A.H.	Presumably he took a photograph of the painting.
A.P.	Yes, I know, but that's what you are talking about.
A.H.	Yes. I feel that Berlioz didn't really think in symphonic terms. It wasn't his nature to do so. After all he wrote very few works in what we might term sonata-form concept. He didn't write string quartets, he didn't write piano sonatas. Here was the orchestra; it is a marvellous tool, with a fantastic variety of colour, and it was obviously a medium which excited him immensely. Presumably he felt he had to find some sort of inner discipline to control the tremendous surge of musical ideas which was coming out of his mind, so he decided to choose a literary mould to put them in. Now isn't this rather a fallacious idea, as I find it a fallacious idea in Strauss? I adore the sounds of *Don Juan*, I adore the sounds of *Till Eulenspiegel*, but I think that if I have to hang on to the programme, it's a weakness.
A.P.	But you don't have to hang on to the programme. The most blatant case in the past few years has been *Zarathustra* which is now certainly the most popular Strauss piece there is and the records of it have sold into the hundreds of thousands, because of the fact that the first two minutes were used in *2001 Space Odyssey* by Stanley Kubrick. Now that music is absolutely chillingly perfect for what is visually on the screen. However, at first it put me off, because, knowing that the piece was based on the Nietzsche concept, I was hoping that Kubrick was not totally aware of the work's actual literary background. However, if you heard it as simply a collection of sounds, it was the perfect title music for *2001*. Now there are hundreds and thousands of young people who have rushed right out and bought a record of *Zarathustra* and play it

constantly; I know this to be a fact, because I have been in many houses where the kids get through with the new Rolling Stones album and put on *Zarathustra*. They don't know the Nietzsche concept, so the music communicates on a completely different level.

A.H.   Do you feel, though, that there is something more musically reputable about writing a work which is not dependent upon an outside, literary inspiration?

A.P.   I think that if someone like Berlioz or Liszt or Strauss writes a piece of programmatic music and that is the way he gets his particular juices flowing, then it justifies writing programmatic music. I think the result is what speaks.

A.H.   Yet Beethoven certainly felt that pictorial music was a little bit beneath his dignity. He was defensive about the *Pastoral* Symphony for example, by saying that it was "more an impression of the countryside than an actual painting". Of course, at that time there was a lot of very rubbishy descriptive music being written, in which there were naive labels saying *The Sound of the Battle* or the *Cries of the Dying* and that sort of thing. Don't you think that this in itself is an indication that such sources of musical inspiration can be a little cheapening?

A.P.   Well yes, surely. If you really predetermine precisely and exactly what the music is supposed to portray. That is why film music is, ninety-nine and nine-tenths per cent of the time, meaningless without the film and sounds quite trashy.

A.H.   I'm glad you raised the point about film music, because don't you think that in cases like yours and my own, one of the reasons why we have been drawn towards writing incidental music, is precisely because we aren't really good enough composers to be able to work without some outside stimulus or prop of that nature.

A.P.   Yes, of course. It would be foolish not to admit it. Those works that I have written for the concert hall are specifically non-programmatic, such as the two concertos and the string quartet, with the exception of a song cycle, which of course must be programmatic.

A.H.   I think I'm right in saying that neither of us is wholly in sympathy with the music of the avant-garde today. Nevertheless, one must take into account the fact that the situation for the young creative artist in any medium is an enormously difficult one, because we have never been so aware as we now are of the inheritance of the past. In Beethoven's time, for instance, the only music that people were interested in was contemporary music. The situation now is that you can go into a record shop and buy a piece of music from any century you care to name from the fourteenth century onwards, and experience it in your own home. Because of this, the young creative artist is aware, as never before, of how many avenues have already been explored; not only is he aware of it, but every person in the audience is liable to be aware of it. Surely this is a good explanation for the recourse to wild experiment at any cost. Shouldn't the composer today divorce himself from all past experience, and try to break completely new ground?

A.P.   I am not sure that I agree with that because, I don't see where just being different is the equation to being good. Just to make sounds that have not been made before is not all that laudable a musical ambition. It has often been the culmination of a style more than the beginning of a new one that has proven the most valuable.

A.H.   Don't you think there has been an enormous acceleration of the pace of change then? If we look back over the last twenty years there have been fantastic changes of style. I mean, composers like Boulez have even disowned works that they have written within a space of five years and said, "That was completely wrong, let's start again."

A.P.   Stravinsky rather dismissed his early work, didn't he?

A.H.   And yet those are the very works by which he is most likely to continue to be known because they've established a firm hold on the affection of audiences. No matter how often the critics tell us that we should admire the serial works of Stravinsky, audiences remain obstinate in their refusal to prefer them to the colourful and tuneful ballets of the early period.

A.P.   We have a tendency, because things are so speeded up, to talk in terms of decades rather than centuries, and yet look how glibly everyone says, "That is an eighteenth-century piece, that is a nineteenth-century piece." I wonder, in a hundred years, what will be a "twentieth-century piece". We are too concerned about what was the style a few years ago. We are, after all, still in the midst of the twentieth century.

A.H.   We use words like "classical", "romantic", and "modern" very loosely, and normally they are associated with a period of time. I am against this, because they are rather emotional words, which I define rather differently. I have always said that the "classical" composer is someone who serves music as something greater than himself, much as a priest serves his God; a "romantic" composer seems to me to use music as a projection of himself. In other words he may write a piece not about love or war or some abstract conception, but

114

about *his* love and about *his* war. The "modern" composer, to me, is someone who is primarily concerned with experiments in sonority. By this definition one might say that Stravinsky, in his middle period, is an extreme example of a "classical composer", Monteverdi is a very "modern" composer, while Debussy stands half way between romanticism and modernity, in so far as the music is both pictorial and personal, but also experimental as far as the artist is concerned.

A.P.   The package that you have just presented is so beautifully tied up that I don't want to undo the ribbon. I mean, we can discuss this for about two days, but it is a very nice thesis.

A.H.   Where I think this is a helpful definition is that it enables us to appreciate elements of all three styles in one and the same composer. In Mozart, for instance, there are aspects of classicism, romanticism and modernity. There are moments when one appreciates the marvellous architectural structure of a movement—his classicism; or in a work like the G minor symphony, one appreciates its intensely romantic character. Then there are times when he uses calculated dissonances in a very "modern" way. Perhaps the reason why Mozart is such a universal composer is precisely because he has his finger on all three of these elements.

A.P.   Mozart to me is a supreme being. I find him to be so much the greatest composer that it is difficult to discuss him in the same terms as anyone else.

A.H.   But if I'm right in suggesting that the reason why a really great composer has a universal following is that he has architectural, emotional and experimental characteristics held in balance, maybe one of the reasons for the poverty of the music of the

	avant-garde today is the fact that they have left out the architectural and emotional elements, and are too preoccupied with experiment.
A.P.	I would agree with you on the lack of architectural sense. However, it must be true that what we deem as totally unemotional is due to our failing, because many people seem very emotionally caught up in it. I have heard pieces that I could only look at surgically, but have seen someone else be incredibly moved, maybe not moved to tears, but affected nevertheless.
A.H.	Stirred up.
A.P.	Yes. You see, what is so marvellous about Mozart is that you can get all three reactions at the one and the same time in the same piece, in the same performance. You get from Mozart's music whatever you bring to it, whether it's sadness or gaiety or profundity. I once conducted the Sixth Symphony of Walter Piston, in New York, and I had done some fooling about with some of his instructions, in the score, and he came backstage and paid me some compliments. Well, with real fear of having slighted that good composer's instructions, I asked him whether he minded my changing the interpretation somewhat. And he said, "Look, there are 3,000 seats in this hall, and with any kind of luck there must have been 3,000 simultaneous and different interpretations of my piece going on." Well I find that a rather profound answer. What I go through when I hear great music is certainly bound to be different from the person sitting next to me because we are both unique. Therefore it is an interesting concept that all the people who have ever heard, let us say the G minor Mozart, have had millions of personal interpretations. Why do we quarrel when we hear one that does not conform with our own?

A.H.   Well, the composer who commits his music to tape in the hope of eliminating the performer altogether would certainly disagree with you. It's very simple to reduce music to its basic essentials. It has pitch and rhythm and harmony, and that's about it. But I have always felt that the obsession with sound for sound's sake is a little bit misleading, because a single note on a clarinet, a horn, a violin, or whatever it may be, instantly evokes an emotional response. If you play a note loud and short, it is like a sharp pain; if you play it quietly and sustain it, it produces an aura of peace. Sound establishes an emotional mood so quickly, that I tend to feel the emotional response in music is rather too easily attained. Now a great deal of modern music is conceived in a rather pointillist style; it's really equivalent to a whole series of different nervous stimuli, like shocks from electrodes, which may be sharp or gentle, soothing or painful. Reducing music to this sort of level seems to me to take away so much of value. The idea of progressing through a series of episodes which lead to a culmination of experience is being sacrificed completely.

A.P.   Yes, but on the other hand, I wonder if it isn't wrong to use comparisons quite so much with other kinds of music. Forgive me for again using a personal example, but it is the best way I can make myself clear. When I did the Penderecki *Hiroshima Threnody* in Houston, Texas, for which I should get some kind of medal, because it was considered quite radical there to do Ravel, I gave a little speech to the audience in which I said, "This piece is not written down as normal music is written down", and I showed them the score, or rather that notation of his which is so wonderfully calligraphic.

A.H.	You could frame it and hang it on the wall it is so pretty.
A.P.	Yes. And I said, "Since it is not written down like normal music, I beg you not to listen to it like normal music. Don't compare it, to last week's Dvorák, or next week's Stravinsky, but imagine for the length of this piece, which is less than ten minutes, that this is when music starts. Try to clear your head for a moment of comparisons." Well of course I was asking the impossible, but I wanted to make them aware at least that this piece was not in direct competition with the *Pathétique* symphony. Probably you and I should figure that there are a whole new set of standards which we are simply too retrogressive to understand at the moment.
A.H.	When you talk about music like this, you are still closing your eyes to one aspect of it which I find rather desperate : surely, never before in the history of music has there been a time when composers have made such a deliberate and self-conscious attempt to cut themselves off from the past. Beethoven accepted the inheritance of Haydn and Mozart gladly enough until he could make something more of it. Even the revolutionaries who really started to break away at the beginning of this century, leading figures like Stravinsky, Bartók and Debussy, each one started by trying to continue the traditions of the nineteenth century. They didn't just simply say, "To hell with the past, it is no good", and then start with a completely new slate. Now is it healthy to do this? Isn't the modern composer throwing out the baby with the bath water?
A.P.	I really have very little to add to that except the following : never before has the composer seemed to want to alienate the audience as much as he

does now. Now, I think it is admirable in the highest sense when a composer, a serious composer, says, "I don't care who likes this and who doesn't, because I know that what I am writing is the essence of me." That is the Beethoven creed and it is beautiful; but I think that there are several of the more militant new composers who have gone one step beyond that. They say, "I don't want anybody to like it." Now that is a different story altogether. There's an enormous difference between, "I don't *care* if anyone likes my music" and "I don't *want* anyone to like it". You could pursue this even a step further, and then it becomes wonderfully ludicrous. You've had pieces actually published which are blank manuscript paper; no notes written down, no music to be played, but published as composition just the same. You must know the piece by John Cage to which I refer. Well, the next step would be for the composer just to sit at home *thinking* about writing a piece, and then perhaps later, an audience could just pretend to have heard it.

A.H.   It's like the famous Webern story, isn't it.

A.P.   Tell me.

A.H.   Oh, there was a group of people who were supposed to be rehearsing a work by Webern, and it was all very, very quiet and very, very fragmentary. There they were, playing these little tiny notes—all whimpers and moans; at one point, a player held up his bow and said, "Maestro, there is an instruction here that I don't understand. You have written *pensato* over this note," and Webern is supposed to have replied, "That means that you don't play note, you just *think* it."

A.P.   You see, my joke is already old! In Germany there is an annual festival of modern music, in a place called Donau-Eschingen. A few years ago they gave the première of a piece for Conductor Alone. By that I mean that a conductor came out on stage, mounted the rostrum, opened a score, and meticulously conducted his way through it, metre changes and all. However, there was no one sitting in front of him, no one played an instrument, there was no noise of any kind. But the piece was done seriously, received seriously, and reviewed seriously, as a legitimate composition. How wonderful to be that composer; he must be up to opus number 1000 by now.

A.H.   Can we turn now to improvisation? As a jazz musician, you obviously have to be an expert in improvisation, because it's the essence of jazz. Now we know perfectly well that there was a great classical precedent for improvisation in the period of Bach, Handel or Mozart. Every composer improvised, even up to Liszt's time.

A.P.   . . . as a matter of course.

A.H.   For some reason, it dropped out of concert music more or less entirely, except for organists; and then it came to life again in jazz. Yet nowadays, the composer is tending to abjure responsibility for his work, putting more and more back into the performer's hands. He says, "Here is an idea"— it may only be a few notes or it may even be a pattern on the page but he says, "Take this and do with it as thou wilt." Now is the composer simply putting the clock back to where it once was, although perhaps to a greater degree, or is he in fact admitting that he no longer has anything to contribute?

A.P.   I don't know what goes on in the mind of a composer who writes what is ninety per cent aleatory. I am simply confessing my ignorance. It is the same as here where we are; a few minutes ago one of the hotel staff here talked to me in Romanian and could not talk any of the other languages I speak, and I therefore did not know what she was getting excited about. That doesn't mean that I disagree with her, because I never understood what she said. That's roughly how I feel about totally aleatory pieces.

A.H. But you could get the drift of what she was saying from the tone of her voice. You could have told whether she was wildly in love with you and wanted to get into bed with you, or whether in fact she was very angry with you for making unreasonable demands.

A.P. Well, in point of fact she seemed quite angry with me, but that isn't enough because I don't know what she was angry about. But when I hear a piece by Lukas Foss, whom I absolutely adore as a human being, I don't know whether to laugh or cry, or try to have him arrested, or committed, or given a medal, because I don't know what caused the piece. It is in a language, in a vocabulary which is absolutely foreign to me, so I cannot have an opinion because it would be so stupid of me to attempt to have one.

A.H. Well, let me just take you up on something which seems a fairly logical follow-on: Let us take a tune like *Summertime*. Now this is a classic tune; it has a marvellous melody, and I'm sure that Gershwin felt that its emotional mood was fixed and absolute. Yet jazz musicians will take a piece like that and totally alter it, playing it at three times the tempo that Gershwin intended, with a very strong cross-beat rhythm which must be totally alien to the original emotional concept in the composer's mind. Only last night, I heard a small band in a café starting up with a very quick, rhythmic version of *Blue Moon* which outraged

	me much more than it does to hear a Bach concerto on a Moog synthesizer.
A.P.	Yes, but I wonder if you had heard *Blue Moon* played double time by a great player whether it would have outraged you, or whether you would not have been struck with his invention.
A.H.	No, I would still be outraged because if I had written *Blue Moon* myself, I would loathe somebody to do that to it, just as I would loathe somebody to play the slow movement of the *Pathétique* sonata as a gay presto.
A.P.	As an ex-jazz player of some experience, let me try to justify it. Most popular songs are judged and remembered by their melody line and by their lyrics. Let's take *All the things you are* as an example. If you ask anyone if they remembered the song, they would in all likelihood either sing or whistle the melody to you. But if you were to ask a jazz musician, "How does *All the things you are* go?" he would answer you, "It goes F minor 7, B flat minor 7, E flat 7, A flat", because those are the harmonies on the first few measures of the piece on which he would then improvise. That same theory holds true on a very fast, mechanical tune or a languorously pretty one. It's simply a different responsibility, a different point of view. The jazzman will admire the tune in its original fashion and admire the harmony, I mean the melodic structure and all that it implies, but then he will simply use that which is the tool to his trade.
A.H.	I know; but I still find that it upsets me when the tune itself is made to undergo such a violent distortion of its original emotional quality.
A.P.	Suppose you were to hear very good jazz players improvise on *All the things you are*, at a very fast tempo, and suppose no one ever stated the melody, even at the beginning, but simply played

endless improvised choruses. The chances are that unless you were practised at listening to jazz you would never realize that it was *All the things you are*, but simply some terrific improvising on given harmonies, and therefore you wouldn't be offended. Improvised jazz is much more the performer's art than the composer's. Some very great jazz musicians almost purposely chose lesser tunes, in order to show off their own improvisatory skill. However, the leaning on the "standard" tunes is going a bit out of fashion; I would say that three-quarters of the jazz you hear today is actually composed by the players themselves, so that would help assuage your sense of outrage.

A.H. Let me suggest a paradox. It seems to me that today we find some composers, of a supposedly serious kind, increasingly passing on the responsibility for their music to the performer, who is given instructions rather than notes to follow. Meanwhile, the jazz performer, who used to rely entirely on improvisation, is turning more and more towards written music, which is a denial of the tradition of jazz. Isn't it possible that the serious composer has been so impressed by the power of improvised music that he has come to say, "Well okay, chaps, you can do it better than I can, so take over from me"; whereas the jazz composer has become so influenced by the sophistication of serious music that he admits that he can never hope to improvise with as much architectural strength, therefore he turns to the written note? Are we not in fact seeing a slow reversal of a kind?

A.P. I'm not sure of my answer. You may be right.

A.H. I am not too concerned about that either. I am much more interested in what you think the future trends will be; because if you are out of

	sympathy with aleatoric music, and if composers in the future are going to write more and more of it, what are you going to conduct?
A.P.	It may well be that more and more composers will find the symphony orchestra too unwieldy, too inexact, and too inopportune to come by.
A.H.	Too predictable in sound ; the sound is blanketed with an aura of tradition.
A.P.	Maybe all that will keep them from writing for the symphony orchestra, but I must say it is going to take centuries for concert-going audiences to feel that way. I don't think that the music that I involve myself in day after day is going to go out the window.
A.H.	I was at a music club not long ago and a man who I should think was about sixty-five came up to me and said, "I don't really know much about music, I am just an amateur listener ; but I am seriously trying to educate myself." And then he said, "I have been listening to a lot of this Stockhausen stuff lately. I don't understand it at all, but I must say it makes Webern seem very tuneful."
A.P.	Well that was a highly intelligent man.
A.H.	I thought it was a very nice remark, but it does show that more people than perhaps you and I would imagine are trying to come to terms with modern music. The fact is that the new generation, the young people, don't find it difficult. You and I may find it difficult because we have been brought up to speak a particular musical language and think in a particular musical way ; when we write music, there are certain harmonies which come instinctively to our fingertips and then flow out through our pens. If people haven't got this preconception, Stockhausen doesn't present such difficulties.

A.P.   But unless you've been brought up in a musical vacuum, you're bound to have preconceptions! The whole attitude of the audience to contemporary music has changed. In previous centuries, when there was an impending première of Brahms, or Beethoven, or Verdi, the anticipatory excitement was boundless. And I am referring to non-professionals, just listeners. The same people who, in today's society, might look forward to a new Elliott Gould movie, looked forward to an important musical première then. You cannot tell me that there are large groups of people in England who are already saying "Oh boy, Peter Maxwell Davies's new opera will be staged next year", and in America they're not saying, "I hope that Aaron Copland's new work will be played in a city easily accessible to me", and yet it is precisely that kind of enthusiasm which used to be prevalent in other days.

A.H.   Yes, but you are arguing against yourself in a way because, while they might not want to go and hear the new Aaron Copland piece, you have only got to advertise the first performance of a new Stockhausen work to sell the house out.

A.P.   There will always be big enough cults to sell out a few houses for a few years. There are enough fans of Havergal Brian in England right now to warrant a sold-out night at the Albert Hall, but not enough to make him part of the normal season's repertoire. Stockhausen—and when I say Stockhausen, I am using his name as a symbol, not specifically—is a great influence and will bring large crowds to various festivals. But these festivals still are outer-circle, *dernier cri* efforts and don't influence the mainstream of audience thinking.

A.H.   But could there be such cult figures, could they

have this enormous drawing power, if in fact the music they produce is not truly valid?

A.P.   Ah, but if I knew that I would be running the world, wouldn't I.

A.H.   We have been fairly honest about admitting our own failings as well as perhaps being a little immodest about our successes ; but can I ask you a completely frank question? You know in your heart, just as I know in mine, that neither of us is a composer of stature ; why do you compose, if you know your music is not going to be played in a hundred years' time?

A.P.   Because it gives me pleasure.

A.H.   That's a good reason.

A.P.   It gives me pleasure to write. I don't have the kind of compulsion to write that a genius does. The ideas do not wake me at three in the morning and give me a sharp kick and say, "Here is a great theme", or idea or whatever. But I am a professional musician, and I have had to compose for both commercial and other reasons. I am not constantly with pen and paper simply because I don't have the drive to do it. But it gives me great personal satisfaction to write the piece and have it played. And I never kid myself that it is for posterity. I would be satisfied for it to be for the week after next, but when I have finished a work, such as the cello concerto, such as the song cycle, the guitar concerto, I have a sense of well-being, and if it then is played, chances are I will learn something from it, and I will file that away and see if I can use it next time, and it is an almost purely selfish reason.

A.H.   You had a very nice reason, I thought, a very *proper* reason for writing the cello concerto.

A.P.   The reason was that I had just been appointed the principal conductor of the Houston Symphony and we had a wonderful principal cellist, who was about to be wooed away from us by the Cleveland Orchestra, where the salary was greater. I didn't want to lose the principal (it was a woman, Shirley Trepel, an absolutely brilliant cellist) and I said, "I tell you what, if you stay I will write you a cello concerto to give as a première next year." She said, "Are you serious?" and I said, "Absolutely", and I knew also that she would not play solos in Cleveland, to the extent that I could offer. It so amused her, that someone would actually write a concerto in order to keep her in Houston, Texas, that she said, "Well, fine", and she signed a new contract with the orchestra. I kept my word and that summer I wrote her a cello concerto. Now I find that a very valid reason to write one. It actually meant that it would be played right away.

A.H. It's a reason which Bach would have appreciated very much.

A.P. Well, I wish Bach had been the conductor and composer in question, and I could have just listened to it. One of my favourite music stories is apropos here. A young composer came to Brahms and asked if he might play for the master a funeral march he had composed in memory of Beethoven. Well, permission was granted, and the young man earnestly played away. When he was through, he sought Brahms's opinion. "I tell you," said the great man candidly, "I'd be much happier if you were dead and Beethoven had written the march."

Anyway, I often want the pleasure of composing something, but I much prefer it to be for a specific purpose. Douglas Cummings, our LSO principal cellist, has now asked me for a piece; I recently wrote two short pieces for Itzhak Perlman. Ashkenazy asked me for some piano preludes. All these I am flattered and happy to work on. But I do like it when the pleasure I derive from writing is spurred on by some practical reason. Not money, I hasten to add, but a definite performance.

A.H. I feel this very much because I am not concerned with writing works for posterity. Posterity isn't going to be interested. But I have found someone who appreciates my writing for them, and that is young people. I have written quite a number of works now for young people, precisely because I feel that they need something from me and I can give it to them—just as I have written small-scale operas because I think this is something that I can do well. I feel that the problem of communication between audience and composer can be largely solved if composers will write for young people and not be too remote. The discipline of having to limit oneself to the technical abilities of the young, gifted though they are, means that the composer has to stop himself from getting too fanciful. Of course I am not alone in this; Benjamin Britten, Richard Rodney Bennett and Malcolm Williamson have all written substantial works for young people. Do you think that in the future, people are going to look back, and say that ours was a period in which suddenly composers took an interest in large scale music for the young?

A.P. It seems a sweet and happy thought but I never have considered it before. However, I don't see why not. It seems an awfully good idea, a well thought out and intellectually possible idea, so I don't see why it couldn't come about, but I haven't noticed a trend, to tell you the truth.

A.H. Well, there is one there. I would love to feel that in fifty years' time every composer would regard it as part of his duty to the world to communicate through children, and to use children as a means of expressing ideas which were not in any way childish.

A.P.   I think the whole idea is absolutely beyond reproach. But if your contention is true that the future generations having grown up on Stockhausen will be totally used to it, then the music for children of future generations will be even wilder than the music for grown-ups now.

A.H.   Well I see no harm in that.

A.P.   Neither do I. But what relieves me immensely is that I won't have to conduct it.

A.H.   What I feel is important about this is that there is an entire new group of people who have never been available to composers before. Youth orchestras didn't exist in the nineteenth century. Beethoven didn't write music for youth orchestras because there weren't any. So is this not a phenomenon which is going to become increasingly important as music becomes an increasingly important part of the school life of every country in the world?

A.P.   Yes, and therefore, the fact that the bells are supposedly tolling the death knell for the symphony orchestra seems to me to be premature. If there is in our time a twentieth-century phenomenon known as the youth orchestra, then it stands to reason that there will be a twenty-first century symphony orchestra.

POSTLUDE

André Previn

When I first came to England, I was ill-equipped to cope. I panicked at driving on the left side of the road, I had never conducted Elgar, I couldn't understand cricket rules, I was unaware that pubs close during the day, and, forgive this confession, I didn't know who Tony Hopkins was. I quickly found out that, in order for me to take my place in the musical community, this last ignorance was the worst. My first introduction to him came when I bought a book of his essays while browsing through the shelves at Hatchards. I was impressed with his erudition and with his direct and uncomplicated approach to music. I liked the book a lot. Then I began hearing his broadcasts, and my respect grew. Here was a deft and informed voice on music, making it interesting and palatable to professionals and laymen alike. But I never set eyes on him before the day Jamie Hamilton invited us both to lunch in order to propose this book. By that time, I had formed my own mental picture of him. Obviously he was tall and spare, with deep-set Huxley eyes; he would dress in somewhat baggy pin-stripes, with his school tie narrowly knotted. Well, Mr. Hopkins was quite a surprise. He is short and bustling, extrovert and funny, and usually dressed in Mick Jagger's cast-offs. That's on his serious days. Well, we got on together very well, and I looked forward to his coming along on part of the LSO's Balkan tour.

All the conversations which make up this book were taped within the space of one week, in spare hours between concerts and rehearsals. We laughed a great deal, and, I'm afraid talked a good deal of nonsense. We have tried to eliminate the worst of the nonsense from the book, but I suppose there is still a little something to offend everybody. At first, I attempted seriously to rewrite a lot of it. Musical theorizing is not at its best when done in the airport waiting-room in Cluj, Romania, with the cassette tape-recorder coming in for its share of suspicious glances from the ever-present guards. Another reason for possible revisions was that in the seven months interim I have had certain musical experiences which could conceivably alter some of the opinions I expressed. But then, on second thought, I decided against radical alterations. This book should remain exactly what it was meant to be in the first instance ; the conversations of two professionals in love with music. Not planned essays or researched articles ; just random opinions and recollections. So I contented myself with straightening out some syntax and correcting some of the most endearing typing mistakes I have ever seen. I don't envy anyone the task of transcribing endless reels of tape on to paper, especially when the hours of talk all concern a specific subject not familiar to most typists. It became a great game to decipher that "Brooklyn" was the typist's distortion of Bruckner, "Molly" was Mahler (think about that one), "Pheasant" was Voisin, and that the name Brahms did not denote two or more members of the family Brahm. I think a rather good question for future music exams might be "What ARE Brahms?"

Anyway, I am now, six years after my arrival in England, better suited. I now drive with insolence, have conducted a great deal of Elgar, I know exactly when to visit my local, and, best of all, I made friends with Tony Hopkins.

But cricket still baffles me.

DATE DUE

GAYLORD   PRINTED IN U.S.A.